WHAT A TIME
TO BE ALIVE!

WHAT A TIME TO BE ALIVE!

REINSTATING THE AMERICAN DREAM THROUGH PASSIVE INCOME AND TINY LIVING

AUSTIN LAUDENSLAGER

Published by Best Seller Publishing®, Pasadena, CA

Best Seller Publishing® is a registered trademark

Printed in the United States of America.

ISBN 9798681801504

For more information, please write:

Best Seller Publishing®

253 N. San Gabriel Blvd, Unit B

Pasadena, CA 91107

or call 1(626) 765 9750

Visit us online at: www.BestSellerPublishing.org

Table of Contents

DEDICATION

To my parents. You have always been my inspiration and the light at the end of the tunnel. Thank you for teaching me that persistence pays. Thank you for giving me the time and attention that a child needs to grow up without self-induced limitations. Thank you for teaching me that I can do anything I set my mind to do. And thank you for showering me with the unconditional love and consistent consequences I needed to become who I am today.

I hope holding this book gives you both immense satisfaction, knowing how much you've sacrificed to give me every opportunity you possibly could throughout my entire life—after all, it's your story too.

Austin Laudenslager
April 2020

My Source of Inspiration

I awoke to the sound of my alarm; something I wasn't used to anymore. It was 4:00 a.m. on a cold Monday morning, and I was alone in the central mountains of New Zealand's north island. I got my photography gear together, stowed all the items that could roll around inside my rental van, and set off for the short drive to the base of Mount Tongariro. I had planned to be one of the first people on what is considered to be the world's greatest single-day hike: the Tongariro Alpine Crossing. This was the main attraction—the thing that I was most looking forward to on my two-week solo photography tour of the north island. I was beyond pumped to photograph the three crazy-colored volcanic lakes beyond the high alpine area, and I couldn't wait to get started on the trail and finally see them for myself.

I took off well before the sun rose and, as planned, was one of the first people on the trail. I had prepared well for the "strenuous" rated 19.4 km roundtrip hike. I had cold weather gear, a headlamp, plenty of snacks and water, my tripod and photography gear, and a companion you probably wouldn't expect (more of him shortly). This was no vacation; this was my new everyday life. Only three months prior, I had decided to completely redesign my life and switch from unfulfilled corporate cog to full-time digital nomad. Why? Because I ran the numbers dozens of times and realized I could still achieve the same financial results if I made a relatively small amount of money but minimized my cost of living. By looking at my options quantitatively, I concluded that if the financial progress were equal in both scenarios (full-time unfulfilled work vs. full-time digital nomad), I should proceed with the option that would bring me the most joy, satisfaction, and fulfillment. I thought, Why sacrifice my youth working 12- to 14-hour days when I could achieve the same net income in a much more enjoyable way? I found a way to save the same amount of cash on a yearly basis while working much less and doing the things I wanted to do while still young and able. This exercise made it an easy change to justify.

While this cold, early Monday morning wakeup made for a strenuous day, it was one thousand times better than any Monday sitting in my old office. It wasn't just the giant unearthly volcano, old lava fields, or stunning volcanic lakes that made this day special, it was my companion. My companion didn't miss a step. I didn't have to wait on him a single time, he never complained, and he proved to be just the mentor I had been searching for. He was utterly weightless, refreshingly innovative, and we are cut from exactly the same cloth. A match made in heaven. At the time, my companion was the only person in the world I could honestly say I envied. I didn't envy his wealth; I envied his meaningful work, his thirst for ultimate freedom, and his strong desire to make a positive impact on others. My companion was Tim Ferris—not in person, but in audiobook format. For 19.4 kms, I listened to Tim's *The 4-Hr Workweek: Escape 9-5, Live Anywhere, and Join the New Rich*, and by the end of it, I too was weightless—soaring, actually. In fact, I ran almost the whole way down the mountain. This was partly to avoid a parking ticket, and partly because I couldn't wait to journal about all the ideas and inspiration I'd just gained.

At the time, I had already escaped the nine-to-five and was living wherever I wanted, making money online. But I still needed Tim's guidance, his strategies, his tools and, most of all, his courageous example of what life could be like if you get out of your own way.

Tim opened my eyes to life's true possibilities. Possibilities that are far above and beyond the standard options handed to us through cultural conditioning. Tim gave me two revolutionary ideas that have effectively changed the course of my life:

1. We can create digital products that can be sold in automated fashion, thus producing a consistent income without the need for constant attention.
2. We can leverage our time through automation and virtual assistants, thus freeing our time to spend however we please.

My new life and associated lifestyle are built upon these two innovative ideas.

What a Time to Be Alive! is both the story of why I decided to redesign my life and my own version of Tim's *The 4-Hr Workweek*. In his book, Tim includes many stories and examples of people utilizing his strategies to become what he calls "the new rich"—people rich in free time and liberty. These stories gave me the roadmaps and inspiration to achieve the same end result, but they didn't provide ultra-specific processes, proven online business models, or solutions that I could utilize to become the "new rich" myself. Building on Tim's success and courage, I decided to provide more specific solutions that people can use to gain ultimate freedom and join the new rich. In this book, you'll find two new innovative resources anyone can use to make the changes they desire in life.

So, what happens when someone makes the lifestyle changes they desire? What happens when someone makes a transformation and achieves the financial freedom they intended? Our respective answers to these questions are what separates my book from Tim's. This is where things get exciting. This is where life begins! I'll say that both of our answers are great options, but I won't spoil it for you—I think you'll enjoy figuring it out for yourself. When you do, you'll know deep down which is right for you. I'll give you a hint regarding my answer: instead of aspiring to be in the traditional top 1%, aspire to be in the top 1% of people doing meaningful work.

Tim, thank you for the knowledge, the inspiration, and the courageous example to follow. I couldn't have made it this far without you. It is my sincere desire that people will come to value this book as I value yours.

PART I

The Crisis

CHAPTER 1

A Wrong Turn on the Freedom Trail

NO MAN IS FREE WHO IS
NOT MASTER OF HIMSELF.

Epictetus

★

If we could somehow gather America's Founding Fathers for a round-table discussion today, it wouldn't be exceedingly difficult to explain to them that the majority of Americans are nowhere near living the life of freedom and happiness that the founders intended. There would be a panel dedicated to our widespread chronic stress and unfulfilled workplaces, a panel dedicated to explaining how Americans work their entire lives just to gain liberty for the first time only in old age, and a panel examining how the cost of higher education is crippling America's young people and preventing them from the pursuit of happiness.

The Founding Fathers laid the groundwork of the American Dream in the Declaration of Independence, although the term itself didn't appear until 1931, when it was coined by James Truslow Adams in his book, *The Epic of America*. The Declaration of Independence (1776) is one of the most important documents within the history of

Western democracy because it established the core principles of basic human rights. These inalienable rights—life, liberty, and the pursuit of happiness—are the very core of what became known as the American Dream, although the original intent of the Declaration is different from our perception of these rights today.

In *The Epic of America*, Adams defines the American Dream this way:

> […]*not a dream of motor cars and high wages merely, but a dream of social order in which each man and each woman shall be able to attain to the fullest stature of which they are innately capable, and be recognized by others for what they are, regardless of the fortuitous circumstances of birth or position.*

This description of the American Dream is possibly the most consistent with the intent the Founding Fathers established many years before. It suggests that the American Dream grew from the idea that everyone has the right to become the best version of themselves as possible. Indeed, the U.S. government was initially created to protect this right.

Furthermore, our Founding Fathers introduced the revolutionary idea that each person's desire to pursue their own idea of happiness was not self-indulgence, but necessary to a prosperous society. These visionaries had it correct. But throughout the 20th century and the early part of the 21st century, the foundation they established was lost, forgotten, and widely misused.

THE "DREAM HOME"

In the 1930s, when Adams was writing, the American Dream still had more to do with morality than material success. Today, many say the American Dream is dead, while others think it's defined as the opportunity to acquire material possessions. In any case, most people agree that it somehow revolves around opportunity. A brief look at

American history gives us important insights about how modern Americans perceive the American Dream today. Throughout recent decades, individuals, organizations, the U.S. government, and cultural movements have been using the American Dream as a force to advance their causes, grow their bank accounts, push their ideologies, and promote change.

It's no mystery that the American Dream has been intertwined with politics since the term's first appearance in 1931. Shortly after World War II and the victory over fascism, the American Dream still signified freedom and equality in the hearts and minds of Americans. In 1951, the former chaplain of the U.S. Senate, Peter Marshall, redefined the American Dream spiritually, in combination with the existing ideology of equality and equal opportunity: "Religious liberty to worship God according to the dictates of one's own conscience and equal opportunity are the twin pillars of the American Dream." Shortly after Marshall's redefinition, the term began to appear regularly during the 1960s. This largely had to do with Martin Luther King Jr., the inspiring and powerful leader of the most notable cultural movement our country has ever known—the civil rights movement. In his famous "I Have a Dream" speech in 1963, MLK spoke of a vision that was "deeply rooted in the American Dream": a world without prejudice and hatred; a world that would enable mutual respect for all people, regardless of color, socioeconomic status, and educational level. To me, his main message was that there is just one prerequisite to love and respect—life itself.

Not surprisingly, as the term became more commonplace, its ties to equality and personal potential began to crumble. This was largely due to the rise of modern marketing. The deterioration of the true American Dream began to accelerate in the 1970s and '80s, when home builders found they could exponentially grow their bank accounts by marketing the American Dream as synonymous with homeownership. Their message was that to be a "true citizen," one must uphold the vision of the country and either buy or build a home. This was one of the more influential forces that helped derail the Dream from the track laid by our revolutionary Founding Fathers. At this point, the American Dream was widely accepted to be more associated with materialism than the values set forth in the Declaration of Independence. Notably, homebuilders weren't the only ones to see this opportunity and capitalize financially. Increasing home sales quickly became an integral part of public policy because governments recognized it was a mode of economic stimulation, and every U.S. president naturally wants to be responsible for increased prosperity.

Government officials have been promoting homeownership since President Franklin D. Roosevelt created his Economic Bill of Rights in his 1944 State of the Union Address. He defined the pursuit of happiness as decent housing, a good job, education, and healthcare. Immediately following FDR's plan came President Truman's Fair Deal, which expanded the Dream to include entitlement. This meant that if you worked hard and played by the rules, the government would do its best to guarantee a home, financial security, healthcare, and education.

Once the 1990s began, technology reinforced the marriage between materialism and the American Dream more than anyone could've anticipated. Americans began craving their own personal computers, televisions, cell phones, and anything else with a substantial marketing budget. Shortly after the 2000s, consumerism spiraled out of control … until September 29, 2008, when the stock market crashed and the subprime mortgage crisis emerged, reinforcing the fact that we were in a major global recession due to our reckless habits. Consequently, the Great Recession weakened the widespread materialistic mindset and made us second-guess what we wanted the American Dream to be. But not everyone has changed their tune yet.

In the 2000s, many national leaders have continued to shift the Dream back toward homeownership, as promoted by FDR and Truman. These values, pushed down from the top, not only affect major government decisions on housing, regulations, and mortgage guarantees, but affect millions of private choices, including whether to buy an extravagant home, rent an apartment, or start a business. In a speech in January 2017, President Trump claimed that "the American Dream is back." Together with Secretary of Housing and Urban Development Ben Carson, Trump suggested that the American Dream equates to owning a beautiful home and a roaring business. Later that same year, in a speech at the National Housing Conference, Carson outright claimed that homeownership is a central part of the Dream by saying that he "worries that millennials may become a lost generation for homeownership, excluded from the American Dream."

On one side, we have the same vision of homeownership from the 1970s and '80s being sold to the public, while on the other side, a large portion of the population has been forced to recognize the possible perils associated with that version of the Dream. Because of this, according to reports in *The Washington Post*, 48% of millennials argue the American Dream is dead—merely a thing of the past. And per *Inc.* Magazine, 94% of millennials say their number-one goal in life is not a fulfilling career or to find love, but to be debt-free. Personally, I find this goal very saddening. Contrary to popular belief, we don't need a new dream; we simply need to reinstate the original.

To eliminate confusion and our collective misunderstanding, allow me to reinstate the American Dream in simplistic modern terms: **The American Dream is having our basic human needs met so we can focus on the things that are most meaningful to us and gain the opportunity to work towards our individual and collective potential.**

As you'll see as this book progresses, the American Dream is in fact alive and well, and more prolific than ever before. We have a unique opportunity before us to finally claim the society that our Founding Fathers designed for us. It begins with recognizing our individual and collective potential. To do this, we must reshape our understanding of what's humanly possible in the 21st century and appreciate all we have been blessed with.

The potential of a single person is greater than it has ever been. Due to the tools at our fingertips, each of us is positioned to do more and to be more than most of the people who came before us. Despite recent trends, for the first time in human history, it's possible for a person to choose to move up in socioeconomic class because, more than any generation before us, we now have the tools to leverage our most important resource—our time.

The American Dream is a corrective force, which means that when society starts to fall away from the foundation our forefathers established, the people stand up to fix it armed with the power of the American Dream. In the 20th century, America witnessed many social movements demanding access to the power of the American Dream— women, workers, African Americans, seniors, and welfare recipients, to name just a few. You'll find that I am utilizing similar tactics in *Part I—The Crisis* to combat widespread chronic stress, unfulfillment and the household debt crisis. After that, in *Part II—Multiple Passive Income Streams*, I'll offer new and creative solutions to help you eliminate any form of debt quickly and grant you the opportunity to spend your time however you choose. I wrap it up in *Part III—Tiny Living* with a game-changer that might enable you to retire earlier than your wildest dreams.

The main goal of this book is to show that you have alternative life options. There is no longer a need to settle for an unfulfilled existence or a toxic work environment. I want you to know that it's always possible to change your life and begin working to become who you know deep down you can be. My hope is that these words enable you to understand there is nothing stopping you living your version of an extraordinary life but you. I offer my story not to attract attention, but to light the way for people that come to value their time more than the money and material possessions we have been conditioned to serve.

This goes out to all the people continually telling themselves that there has to be more to life than this and there has to be a better way to make money. I'm here to tell you that there is so much more than you can conceptualize when you're stuck in the grind. And there are many better ways to make money than trading your time for money somewhere you don't enjoy or get excited about. Like many who came before me, I am using the American Dream for what it's worth—a powerful force capable of creating meaningful change and driving innovation. Throughout this book, I'm going to show you not only how to begin thinking outside the traditional box, but how to get out of the box entirely if you so choose. Only there can we truly begin to innovate and build a better path forward.

As someone who has successfully found my way out of the conventional box, I'd like to formally introduce you to the grand unveiling of my version of the American Dream. It's time to course-correct the American Dream so that it can once again serve its purpose and begin to liberate people from unnecessarily stressed and busy lives and provide the opportunity for people to "attain the fullest stature of which they are innately capable." It is my hope that this book reminds you of the fortitude our great country was founded upon and provides value to you if you're someone who wants to start living your own version of the American Dream by eliminating the need to trade your freedom for money. You have an incredible individual opportunity in front of you to seize everything you ever wanted. Will you capture it or just let it slip?

CHAPTER 2

The Ultimate Freedom

THE SECRET OF LIBERTY IS TO ENLIGHTEN
MEN, AS THAT OF TYRANNY IS TO KEEP
THEM IN IGNORANCE.

Maximilien Robespierre

★

Americans in the 21st century have more rights and freedoms, legally speaking, than any other American population in history. Every one of us has the right to be whoever we want to be and to do whatever we want to do. We are all recognized as a person before the law, we have freedom of belief and religion, we are free to marry and have children, we have the right to own property, we have the freedom to participate in government, we have the right to education, and we have freedom from slavery (as defined by law). I'm not going to list every single freedom everyone has been granted since the Declaration of Independence, but I am going to dissect our most important inalienable rights—life, liberty and the pursuit of happiness, otherwise known as the American Dream. I'm sure you're extremely familiar with these rights, but I doubt you've considered you only truly possess one of them. Congratulations, you guessed it, you have the right to life! To understand the other two rights, it helps to know what our Founding Fathers intended them to mean at the time of their writing in 1776, and what most people believe them to mean 240-plus years later.

Our definition of liberty has largely remained the same, although most people don't know what it means in the context of the Declaration of Independence and don't possess it on a day-to-day basis. Liberty is the ability to do as one pleases. Most people can't fathom what they would do if they had the freedom to wake up each day and do what they wanted because they are too busy doing things they don't want to do in exchange for money. This is surely not the society our Founding Fathers envisioned for us. They wanted us to have the time to follow our personal convictions, passions, and joys. Whether you know what they are yet or not, we all have convictions and passions within us. Our Founding Fathers built liberty into the foundation of our society so that each of us would have the opportunity to make our lives meaningful— to make our lives count.

On the other hand, our definition of the pursuit of happiness has changed greatly since the concept's inception. Our Founding Fathers had a definition of happiness different from the one we do currently. They believed that a happy, well-lived life is one rich in purpose, fulfillment, and *inner* prosperity—that is to say believing in something greater than ourselves while serving the greater good. In other words, they thought of life as the pursuit of *meaning*. Today, cultural conditioning and modern advertising have led us to believe that happiness is born through consumption of material things. We think, *If only I had a bigger house, a better car, nicer clothes, and more things, I would be happy and fulfilled.* This definition of modern happiness is counterproductively perpetuating a cycle of stress, anxiety, exhaustion, and unfulfillment for those who subscribe to it. It has also stripped us of our pursuit of meaning since we are instead pursuing meaningless material possessions and instant gratification.

FINANCIAL FREEDOM AND THE INTERNET

Thankfully, there is a modern solution for obtaining liberty and the pursuit of happiness as it was initially intended. The solution is the ultimate freedom, the only freedom most people still lack. The ultimate freedom is financial freedom—a freedom that will change the world.

Financial freedom is the key that unlocks liberty and the pursuit of happiness. It is of utmost importance in 2020, and it is not being discussed like it should be. We all deeply crave it, but most of us have been convinced by cultural conditioning that it's only for the elite. Fortunately for us, cultural conditioning always gets crushed by innovation one way or another, and the innovation we need to solve this problem already exists! We are not strangers to it; in fact, it's been mainstream for 15 to 20 years now. Some of us grew up with it, some of us adapted to it, and others have already mastered its capabilities and capitalized on its potential. I'm talking of course about the internet. And despite it being something we all take for granted now, I believe the global transformation the internet is facilitating is only just beginning.

Before I truly realized the capabilities of the internet as a means to achieving financial freedom, I was living a life very similar to many people. I was working 50-plus hours each week and living in a young professional's hub in Uptown, Dallas, where things to do consisted of patio drinking and hanging out with friends. At the time, my friend group of about eight guys was very close-knit because we made it a point to get together during the week over a meal to connect with one another before the weekend festivities began … and there was alcohol involved. Most of us are retired NCAA athletes of some sort, so we typically met on Thursday nights at my place to watch whatever sport was on, which was usually the NFL. Meals consisted of grilled steak, garlic bread, and a vegetable of some sort (to make our moms proud). It was during this time that I began to solidify my thoughts on the corporate world, since I lived it all day every day, and my friends were doing the same thing as me at different companies and in different industries.

Through lengthy discussions comparing our jobs, work cultures, industries, bosses, and coworkers, I began to understand that no one knows what they're doing, no one likes what they're doing, and everyone is just there for the money. I saw that the whole corporate system was designed to be just comfortable enough to keep people there and mildly engaged. Some of my friends were bored and didn't have enough to do at work to keep them occupied, while I was on the other end of the spectrum without enough hours in the day to do my job, let alone anything extra. I knew we all made about the same amount of money, but compared to my friends, I realized I was more stressed, anxious, and overworked than they, and had much less freedom.

At this point I began asking everyone I met if they honestly enjoyed what they did for a living. Almost unanimously the answer was no! In only two conversations of the more than fifty I had during the three years I researched this question was the answer, "Yes." Why are people so convinced that unmotivated work is just something we must go through, like it's some rite of passage? Predictably, people attempted to justify their reality by saying things like, "It's supposed to be hard; that's why it's called work." Having heard this from so many people, I bought into it for years. Now I realize that people who think that way are too afraid to lose their comfortable lifestyle in search for more, or they simply don't know that other options exist, or they don't have the energy to figure out an alternative. More often than not, it's all the above. Sadly, the people I just described are not living the American Dream. How can they be? They don't have the time!

THE COST OF "NO TIME"

Not having the time to truly live your life has a compounding effect. Things escalate from "not having the time" to the following:

- Not living an intentional, purposeful, and meaningful life. When you are constantly in a rush, the quality of everything you do suffers. Quality cannot exist without presence.
- Neglecting your mental and physical health.
- Ignorance of your "life numbers"—meaning, not knowing when you'll achieve financial freedom. You can't know what you are working towards if you don't know your numbers. You need to know what you're working towards so you can judge whether the time sacrifice to get there is worth it or not.
- Not evolving and working towards your personal potential.

It's easy to fall into this trap when you spend all your waking hours working on things you don't really care about. I tell you from experience, you often feel tired—not because you've done too much, but because you've done too little of what sparks a light in you. I would come home every day from work exhausted mentally, emotionally, spiritually, and somehow physically even though I sat at my desk for 14 hours. I couldn't find a way to maintain my mental and physical health amidst all the stress and work hours. It was either get up before 5:00 a.m. to exercise before work and have an 18-hour day, or don't exercise at all, because God knows I couldn't get it done after being drained from a full day at the office. I found myself wondering how on earth people work full-time and raise a family. Watching some of the older guys in the company with kids, it didn't take long to realize that they were absent from their children's lives. I saw the hours they were putting in, with frequent travel, and deduced that they might be getting 30 minutes per day with their children, if they were lucky. That is no way to raise a family, and I decided that if I was blessed with a family one day, there was no way I'd be letting other people raise my children. A wise man once said, "A parent's job is to create memories for their children." This takes significant time and attention, and no child will remember all the regular days they spent at home waiting for their parents to come home from work just to get 30 minutes of face time. This realization was one of the final nails in my corporate coffin.

By this time, I'd established that I was overworked and underpaid compared to my peers, I was becoming unhealthy at an alarming rate in multiple ways, and I had zero time to work on myself. I was spending all my time and energy at a place that was slowly crushing my soul and it felt like I had sold my life for financial gain even though I actually had negative wealth due to my student loan debt (more on that later). Because of the immense pain I was experiencing, I began to crave liberty more than anything in the world, and I knew that the only way to get it was through financial freedom. I hypothesized that with financial freedom, I would have time to focus on things I found meaningful, instead of feeling forced to give my time to the meaningless. I'll admit, at the time I didn't fully comprehend the possible impacts financial freedom could have on an individual. I also didn't truly understand how much I had been neglecting my individual needs in favor of the company's until the company was no longer a factor in my life. To help you understand my thought process, the engineer in me created the equation below:

*The American Dream = Financial Freedom = Liberty =
Being Time-Rich = the Opportunity to Reach One's Potential*

I believe this equation summarizes the intent of our Founding Fathers as it applies to the American Dream today.

The most important thing to understand about financial freedom is liberty. When you have as much money as you need, you don't have to spend ten hours a day trading your time for money; you now have ten hours to do as you please. I call this being time-rich. After making the switch, I know I'd rather be rich in time than rich in money any day. There is a powerful satisfaction and deep sense of gratitude that comes with waking up every day and telling myself, "Everything I will encounter today I've purposefully chosen for myself." Although many of us don't realize it, everyone is working to become time-rich as quickly as possible: it is synonymous with retirement, as well as financial freedom. Thankfully for us, "retirement" doesn't have to be something we put off until old age.

Possessing true liberty creates many possibilities for you to grasp. Becoming time-rich starts with having the time and energy to:

- Process and digest your life choices and current life situation;
- Realize your passions/purpose/value;
- Explore things of interest such as hobbies, topics, and problems you might want to solve;
- Give more of yourself to your spouse, family, friends, children, and community, which enables you to experience more joy and depth in your relationships;
- Change your eating habits;
- Sleep as much as you need to;
- Integrate that game-changing morning and weekend self-care routine (including exercise) you've been wanting to for so long.

Almost miraculously, being time-rich evolves into being able to:

- Produce quality work you are passionate about;
- Travel and experience all that our beautiful world has to offer;
- Eliminate all excuses currently standing in the way of who you are and who you know you can be;
- Create a positive impact in the world.

THE NEXT WAVE OF LEADERS

The next wave of great innovators, musicians, artists, government officials, thought leaders, and philanthropists are going to be products of financial freedom and liberty achieved via the internet. For the first time in human history, we can choose whether we are rich in time or simply another cog in the societal wheel. This is a shocking realization for most and one that deserves appreciation regardless of your personal choice. The more people who achieve financial freedom, the faster we are all going to evolve towards a more sustainable approach towards life on earth. Undeniably, we need more bright and passionate people with a love for humanity who are focused on creating solutions aimed at sustainability, now more than ever. Fortunately for humanity, the motivation for positive impact among millennials is out of this world. According to Forbes, close to 70% of U.S. millennials say that a successful business needs to have a genuine purpose, and more than one-third define success as doing work that has a positive impact on society. Unfortunately, most of them are sitting at a desk in a place they despise, patiently waiting for their paycheck so they can send most of it directly to Uncle Sam to repay their college debt.

At the very core of the American Dream becoming a reality for you lies the freedom to work on the things that satisfy your reason(s) for working. You might be asking, "Isn't that reason to acquire money to pay for the cost of living?" Sadly, this is the case for millions of Americans, particularly millennials, and it is one of the problems I am tackling here. Imagine what your life would look like if your primary focus was not money but something truly meaningful to you. With your basic financial needs met, you would be free to create, free to impact, free to help, and free to evolve. What more could you want?

There is a question I love to ask people to prove this point. While I acknowledge the extremity of the question, there is no denying the relevance if you are someone who wants to live your version of a meaningful life. In a world where work-life balance is seemingly nonexistent, this question can be an eye-opener. When I was at the peak of my corporate career, asking myself this question shook me to my core, lit my inner spirit on fire, and solidified my need for change. It's a simple yes-or-no answer—are you ready? If your employer stopped paying you today, would you show up for work tomorrow? In my opinion, if your answer is no, then you have a serious personal problem: you're effectively wasting your time. If your answer is yes, you probably don't need this book, so go ahead and return to your already divine reality! If your answer is no, I am not suggesting you should not show up for work tomorrow. The question is purely meant to illustrate the need for change. In Parts II and III of this book, you'll discover two different ways to financially justify leaving your job if you so choose.

Throughout history, various social groups have had to fight for freedom: the freedom to speak freely, to bear arms, to dedicate oneself to whatever cause one pleases, to move from one place to another, and so on. Now it's time for us to stand up and fight for our financial freedom. This time, there is no oppressor, no entity holding the power, and no one standing in our way but ourselves. What's stopping us from achieving financial freedom is our current lifestyle choices, our debts, our thirst for material things and, of course, fear. Now that I've introduced the possibility of gaining ultimate freedom through financial freedom and explained some of the life-changing benefits, it's time to dive into some of the specific debts and lifestyle choices that are stopping us from gaining liberty and the opportunity to work towards our individual and collective potential.

The first roadblock, and perhaps the largest, is so deeply rooted in our culture that most people wouldn't even think about attempting to change it. The roadblock is both a lifestyle choice and a massive debt, all in one oversized, unnecessary bundle. I'm talking about mortgages. Ultimate freedom is extremely unlikely in the presence of a typical American mortgage. In the following chapter, I'll explain how most mortgages are financially crippling and totally life-limiting.

CHAPTER 3

Mortgages = Self-Induced Servitude

IT IS DIFFICULT TO FREE FOOLS
FROM THE CHAINS THEY REVERE.

Voltaire

★

I f you're someone who already has a typical American mortgage, you might want to sit down for this. If you're someone who is contemplating buying a house, lock-in because you don't want to miss this. I'm about to expose the traditional American mortgage system and mathematically prove the absurdity most people have signed up for. To do this, allow me to introduce you to Michael and Jessica. Throughout this book, I'll be returning to these two everyday folks to provide real world examples to illustrate my points. Michael and Jessica represent average Americans who have subscribed to the traditional living system and are at different stages in their lives. Their life numbers are no different than the average American's. They are both hard working and do the best they can with what they have.

But before we meet them, let's talk about mortgages. Based on data from the Mortgage Bankers Association, in early 2017 the average mortgage granted in the U.S. was for $309,200 with a payoff term of 30 years. At an average interest rate of 4.1%, a borrower would pay approximately $1,508 per month (in principal and interest) to pay the loan off in 30 years. This does not include utilities, repairs, property taxes, or homeowner's insurance premiums.

It was during this time that our everyman Michael finally saved enough money to put the standard 10% down on his dream home. You should've seen the look on his face when he got his approval for his mortgage loan. He was so proud that he qualified for a $309,200 loan, all he wanted to do was send in his $34,000 down payment and move into his new home. The mortgage broker even told him that his 4.1% interest rate was unbeatable in today's market. Like most Americans, Michael had been told his whole life that the best way to accumulate wealth is through real estate and the first step to becoming wealthy is purchasing your first home. He had no reason to second guess moving forward with his major purchase; after all, this was the plan all along. Michael signed on the dotted line and went on his merry way.

For a moment, set aside the fact that Michael now needs to come up with $1,508 every month for the next 30 years. Like many people, Michael had overlooked a monumental detail—*the total amount to be paid over 30 years*. He was able to justify the $1,508 per month price tag, but he did not realize that his mortgage payments would equate to an extra $233,680 *in interest alone* over the course of his 30-year deal. Paying the minimum cost each month, the total amount paid (in principal and interest) over 30 years would be $542,880! Much different than the $309,200 price tag he thought he was agreeing to. Isn't a 4.1% interest rate supposed to be unbeatable? How does "unbeatable" equate to an extra $233,680? This is the curse of the average American mortgage. Just because you can afford the minimum monthly payment, does not mean you should sign up to pay it. To me, this seems like the exact opposite of building wealth. The reality is that the only group building wealth in this system is the group collecting the interest payments.

I should say that houses do generally appreciate, but not by much more than the annual inflation rate. Due to appreciation, one could argue that at the end of a 30-year mortgage, the net value of the house is greater than the amount of principal and interest the owners paid over the 30-year term. This can be true, but it is a pointless argument unless the owner wants to sell the house and liquidate their asset, and it doesn't take away from the fact that the owner still spent 30-years of their life paying for it.

Now, almost three years into his mortgage, Michael is beginning to realize the harsh reality of his decision because he has only been able to pay the minimum payment each month and so has made nearly no progress on his outstanding balance. He feels like he's spinning his wheels, so he vows to work harder and to do whatever is necessary to make more money so he can make some progress. But how can he make more money? He's already working a full-time job and that's draining as it is. He decides to propose a raise in exchange for additional responsibilities and tasks. To his surprise, his boss agrees, and Michael begins working 50- or 60-hour weeks to meet his new obligations. As much as he loves his house, Michael begins to wonder why he pays so much money for it, since most of his life is spent at work. He is trading five-sevenths of his time (Monday to Friday) for a nice place to sleep and spends two-sevenths of his time (Saturday and Sunday) recovering from the devastating workload he has taken on. Sadly, Michael is not unique. According to the Federal Reserve, mortgage debt in America reached $15.8 trillion in the third quarter of 2019. Accepting an average American mortgage is the single most life-limiting decision one can make in modern times.

On top of the life-limitations of buying an average American house for an individual or family, there are side effects that are further contributing to our generally unsustainable way of living. The size of a new home in the U.S. has more than doubled since 1960 to an average size of 2600 square feet. In the 1960s, even doctors and lawyers in the elite didn't dream of having a house over 2000 square feet. Then, a

1600 square foot house was considered extravagant, but now, 2600 is the norm. I like my space as much as the next person, but according to data released by shrinkthatfootprint.com, Americans have some of the greatest floorspace per capita in the world, with double the residential space of the average European resident. Is it necessary to have double the space per person compared to other developed nations? Americans are living in some of the biggest houses in the world, and the biggest houses in history, and the upward trend isn't slowing down.

SIZE ISN'T EVERYTHING

There are two major negative consequences of our drastic increase in home size. The first is the enabling of a high-consumption lifestyle. Naturally, with more space comes more stuff to fill the space: furniture and décor for every square foot, boxes and boxes of seasonal clutter, and plenty of storage space for whatever else we can justify accumulating. We wouldn't want to feel empty, right? The consumer culture has gotten so out of control, our ludicrous amount of space is already not enough. We now need storage facilities on every block to house all the junk we can't fit in our houses but can't bring ourselves to get rid of. According to the Self-Storage Association, America has more than 50,000 storage facilities, more than five times the number of Starbucks. Currently, there is 7.3 square feet of self-storage space for every person in the nation, so it's physically possible for every American to stand (all at the same time) under the total canopy of self-storage roofing. As if that wasn't crazy enough, statistics reported by the *LA Times* show there are 300,000 items in the average American home.

The second negative consequence of our increase in home size is the amount of energy and materials needed to construct and maintain them. With so much unnecessary space comes unnecessary energy consumption. An average American home runs the heater for half the year and the air conditioner for the other half, and as you know, they don't just heat and cool a room or two, they heat and cool all

2600 square feet of it! Spread this across millions of households simultaneously running their systems, and you begin to understand how we are running out of our traditional energy sources and ruining our environment at the same time.

Remember, ultimate freedom is extremely difficult to achieve in the presence of debt. Because of his decision to accept a massive debt in exchange for an average American home, Michael doesn't have much hope of freedom for the remaining 27 years of his mortgage. Unless he decides to make a change, he's going to spend his remaining youth cooped up working full-time just to pay for a home that he will only use on nights and weekends. Additionally, his hopes of reaching his personal potential will be flushed down the toilet because he's devoted all his time to paying for his house. He has no flexibility living in that cycle besides trading his job for another job and most likely winding up right back where he started.

The perpetual cycle that Michael subscribed to is repeated in millions of homes across America. I believe the stress caused by this cycle is the main contributor to most of our well-known mental health disorders and contributes largely to our widespread poor physical health. According to a recent study by the American Institute of Stress, 48% of people reported sleeplessness due to stress, and 54% of people said stress has caused fights with loved ones. These are troubling statistics that paint the picture of America's love affair with unnecessarily large and expensive homes.

As I alluded to earlier, there is a minority of people who live within this cycle of working full-time to pay for their housing but nevertheless live satisfied and fulfilled lives. These are people that are fulfilling their purpose and chasing their potential through the work they are engaged in full-time. I applaud these people but recognize they are a small minority in today's workplace. However, the purpose of this book is to teach the Michaels out there that two different alternatives can break the cycle and enable you to join the small minority of happy and fulfilled workers.

So, is renting better? Aren't we warned that renting is like pouring money down a drain? Yes and no. Yes, they have a monthly payment to make, which can be just as crippling financially. But no because renters don't have the debt and associated interest to worry about. Also, a renter can (for the most part) walk away whenever they want for a relatively small fee. Fortunately, this was the case when I decided to jump out of the traditional cycle.

Before I began traveling full-time in January of 2019, I had an apartment payment of $1,000/month. I was no different than Michael; I was a slave to my rent payment and my job. I worked full-time to pay for a nice place to sleep and relax on weekends, although I traveled so much for work during the week and for pleasure on the weekends. I found myself wondering why I paid so much for a place I didn't even use since that place was one of the main things that was forcing me to work so hard in the first place. In December of 2018, I sold all my possessions and eliminated my apartment from my life. As hard as it is for people to believe, I now spend less money per year traveling the world and living life on my own terms than I did when I was living and working full-time in Dallas. You'd be surprised how far the $1,000 I used to spend on rent goes now that I have complete freedom and flexibility to be anywhere in the world at any time.

MY MAJOR MORTGAGE DIFFICULTIES

When I was in middle school and early high school, I lived in an average middle-class suburban household. We lived in a big, beautiful house with plenty of space for me, my parents, and my two brothers; we even had a large backyard, which is rare for the cookie-cutter neighborhoods I was accustomed to. We had no reason to question our way of life, since my Dad toiled away day after day, commuting to Dallas and back, which was at least a daily two-hour time-suck in itself. It was easy to take everything for granted when life had always been so good. Then the crash of 2008 struck out of nowhere.

Immediately, my superhero Dad lost his job. Mom worked as a teacher's aide at an elementary school, so she could support us while my Dad found a new job. Months went by, then a year, but still no consistent job for Dad. He was an expert in the health insurance industry and had been working in it for over 20 years. Unfortunately, no one was hiring. I began to see my parents break down from financial stress as my family entered the most arduous period we have ever known. Before we knew it, almost two years had elapsed, and my dad still had no sizeable consistent income. By this time, I was a junior in high school with a little brother below me and a big brother away at college. My parents were warriors during this time. I could tell they were doing everything they possibly could to right the situation and support our family, but they just couldn't get things to go our way. They did everything they could to appear like things were business as usual for me and my younger brother. Then one day, out of sheer desperation, they sat us down for a very sad chat. They needed our help.

My brothers and I had jobs since we were old enough to get them. I had my own curb stenciling business, that had been going since I was twelve, set up with a $250 startup loan from my parents that I paid back with my earnings. I made a few thousand dollars from that business and then sold it to one of my older brother's friends for a ridiculous return on investment a few years later. As a junior in high school, I worked teaching at an afterschool care company, in addition to all my sports and extracurricular activities. I didn't have any spare time available and neither did my little brother, but our family meeting forced us to find some. After that meeting, we were all in it together as a single unit. There were no small contributions. Every dime I made that I didn't need for gas went directly to the family fund so we could pay the mortgage and stay in our home. As my little brother and I were officially recruited to the cause, we gave everything we had. We were then officially introduced to the reality of financially induced stress, depression, and anxiety.

Six months later, my parents had eaten well into their retirement fund and continued to do everything within their power to give us everything they had. I never went hungry a single time, but I sure felt the pressure we were under together. I didn't know it at the time, but each of the last six months we were in that house, we had to borrow $1,500 from friends and family to pay for our mortgage. If not for loving friends, we would've been on the street six months earlier. As a testament to my parent's resourcefulness and the strength of their relationships with friends and family, we somehow scraped by that last six months. Despite our best efforts and help from our loving network, we hit rock bottom. It was time to give up the house: there was no other way to proceed. Because of the housing market collapse, the sale was not favorable. We had to somehow come up with thousands of dollars just to make the deal with a family who got it for a steal. I was very aware of how angry this made my parents. To make matters worse, it wasn't like our income situation had somehow changed with us giving up the house. We had nowhere to go, and no money to get into another home.

I remember this time in my life all too well. It was summertime, and I was headed into my senior year of high school and trying to maintain my status of big man on campus. Almost miraculously, our neighbors to the left offered us rooms in their house for a little while. They were a family of four, but three of them were going away for a few weeks' vacation. Before I knew it, I was sleeping on a bunk bed with my little brother above me. Both of our feet were hanging off the bed due to it being child sized, but we weren't complaining—we knew the alternative. Shortly after we moved out of our old house and into our neighbor's house, the new family arrived with all their things and began moving into the home I'd known for the last five years. It still causes me great pain to think about how hard that was for my family to endure. To our surprise, persistence paid off, and six weeks of tiny bunkbed living later, our church offered us $3,000 so we could pay the deposit on a rental on the other side of town. We officially had a home again.

MY MAJOR MORTGAGE RESOLUTION

As we moved all our belongings for the second time in six weeks from a storage facility into our new rental home, I made a vow I didn't yet know how to honor: I would never be in this situation again. Undoubtedly, the hardest part was witnessing the impact that financial difficulties had on my parents' mental health. Having a front row seat to the suffering, the occasional arguments, the depression, and the frustration caused me to take a long, hard look at how we got into the situation in the first place. I concluded that there had to be a way to eliminate this risk from my life in the future; I just didn't know what it was yet. In hindsight, going through this hardship at a young age was such a blessing. I now know that anyone with an average American mortgage is just one uncontrollable event away from the same terrible financial situation. A person doesn't have control over the housing market or whether they remain employed in an economic collapse. Why put your faith, finances, and prosperity in things you have no control over whatsoever? Especially when it's simply unnecessary to do so anymore.

Before I describe how I achieved my new way of life, we must look at another major hindrance to financial freedom and a life full of liberty. This hindrance is preventing millions of millennials like me from living their versions of the American Dream: it's the student loan. No other generation has experienced this issue quite like we have, and I am determined to do something about it. In the same way that a mortgage forces someone into working full-time, student loans are equally debilitating.

In the following chapter, I'll dissect this widespread issue and shine my light on the pain experienced within the student debt crisis. As you'll see shortly, I went from being a casualty of The Great Recession straight into ground zero of the student debt crisis. As ironic as it is, my intimate involvement in the subprime mortgage crisis pushed me to make the choice to accept student loan debt that immediately put me back in an equally debilitating financial situation. This combination of life events has ultimately caused me to redesign my life in a way that gives me more control over my own prosperity and mental health. Today, I don't have to worry about coming up with $1,500 every month to pay for a bunch of space, I don't have to worry about losing my job, and my faith sure as heck isn't locked up in some silly financial market.

CHAPTER 4

The Student Debt Crisis

NORMAL IS GETTING DRESSED IN CLOTHES
THAT YOU BUY FOR WORK AND DRIVING
THROUGH TRAFFIC IN A CAR THAT YOU ARE
STILL PAYING FOR IN ORDER TO GET TO THE
JOB YOU NEED TO PAY FOR THE CLOTHES
AND THE CAR, AND THE HOUSE YOU LEAVE
VACANT ALL DAY SO YOU CAN AFFORD TO
LIVE IN IT.

Ellen Goodman

America's modern higher education system is based on the idea that an initial investment will produce a return somewhere down the road. This assumes that a person needs a college degree for high-earning potential. For much of the 20th century, this was certainly the case, but the landscape has changed since we've entered the 2000s.

The scale of the debt that exists because of our current education system is second only to American mortgages. According to NitroCollege.com, there is currently over $1.53 trillion of outstanding student loans spread across 44.7 million people. This equates to

1 in 4 Americans between the ages of 20 and 59. In May 2019, the average American bachelor's degree recipient began their journey into adulthood with $37,172 of debt associated with their initial investment in their higher education. This average beginning debt number has increased $20,000 in the last 13 years alone. This means that our average college graduates are starting their lives at a severe financial deficit, in negative wealth! A key indicator that represents the collective progress Americans are making on repayment is the mean debt for all people with outstanding student loans. This value is currently $32,731, meaning that the outstanding debt is mostly concentrated within the cohort of recent graduates. It also shows that even the people who have been faithfully paying their loans for ten or more years have not made much progress on their outstanding balance. This is surely a terrible recipe for life, liberty, and the pursuit of meaning.

One of the main reasons student loan debt has ballooned over the past few decades is because the cost of higher education has risen much faster than incomes. The cost of higher education at both public and private universities has been tracked by the College Board since 1971. In 1971, the average total cost of one year at a public university was $1,410. That equates to 15.6% of the median household income of $9,027, which was manageable for families to pay without going into debt. By 2018, the average cost of one year at a public university was $21,370. That is 34.8% of the median household income of $61,372, which is much less manageable for families to afford without going into debt. Therefore, more than 70% of current graduates are beginning their adult lives with a great personal financial deficit to overcome. So, why are our young people continuing to handicap themselves financially? I believe it's because they don't understand the consequences of the decision to accept student debt until they're already drowning in it and it's too late.

Think about the primary influences on a young person who is thinking of going to college: parents, grandparents, teachers, and high-school sports coaches. Generally speaking, these are people who graduated college before the 2000s began. These are people who grew up with the ideal that a college degree is necessary to achieve the American Dream. Truthfully, most of these people have no idea how limiting it is to begin life with a debt of $37,172 right out of the gate because that was not the case for them. They went to college when the return on investment math still made sense, but they haven't changed their tune because "go to college" is all they know. If they truly understood the numbers and fiscal consequences associated with attaining an average higher education today, I don't think they would be as enthusiastic about promoting it.

If you're a reader debating whether to go to college, my advice to you is to understand the financial aspects of your college choices, and then only seek advice from people who took on similar debt amounts to those you are considering. Additionally, know that you can get an MIT (yes, that MIT) education for FREE. In fact, anyone in the world with access to the internet can. From the MIT OpenCourseWare website: "OCW covers the entire MIT curriculum and includes every MIT department and degree program ranging from the introductory to the most advanced graduate level. Many courses also have complete video lectures, free online textbooks, and faculty teaching insights." MIT is offering their entire catalog of courses to the world for free and empowering individuals to educate themselves by providing cutting-edge tools, resources, and information straight from their classrooms. Quality education that doesn't require decades of debt and freedom forfeiture—what a concept! Note: OpenCourseWare is not a degree granting or credit-bearing initiative, but in my eyes, it's not the piece of paper that matters, it's the education and what you do with it.

Take Steve Jobs for example. He dropped out of Reed College but hung around for another 18-months as a drop-in student before he really quit. The minute he dropped out, he stopped attending the required classes that didn't interest him and began dropping in on the ones that looked far more appealing. In 2005, Steve Jobs delivered the commencement address at Stanford. During his speech, he said that following his curiosity and intuition during his drop-in days proved priceless later on. One of the classes he sat in on was a calligraphy class where he learned about serif and san serif typefaces, about varying the amount of space between different letter combinations, and about what makes great typography great. He found it fascinating but, at the time, thought none of it had a practical application in his life. But, ten years later, when he was designing the first Macintosh computer at Apple, it all came back to him. He designed it all into the Mac. It was the first computer with beautiful typography. Steve Jobs didn't have the piece of paper that told someone he knew calligraphy. He had what actually matters—the education and the desire to do something great with it.

THE MILLENNIAL CRISIS

To begin our modern higher education investment analysis, let's turn to our dear friend, Jessica. Jessica graduated in the top 25% of her high-school class and has always showed great potential. When she was a young girl, she had a passion for helping others. Her teachers noticed she was often the first person to offer a hand to someone in need, regardless of the situation or social status of the person. The fact that she had a "big heart" appeared regularly on her report cards and evaluations. In high school, she put everything she had into getting into a reputable college, since she was told from the time she could walk that there was no other way to be successful in the job market. She had a deep desire to make her parents, teachers, and mentors proud, and she didn't want to be a social outcast by not going to college. Because of this, she enrolled at the university she thought was the best fit for her evolution and enjoyment.

As she got closer to making the decision about what to study, her heart wanted to pursue something in the nonprofit sector, but her mind quickly discovered that business majors make much more money. Eventually, she buried the desires of her heart and headed towards a degree that would give her a quicker return on investment. Her decision was heavily influenced by the fact that she would be taking out student loans to pay for college. This terrified her, but everyone else was doing it, so she thought it couldn't be so terrible. After all, she had been groomed for college her whole life, why would she back out now?

Jessica graduated college in May 2019 with a bachelor's degree in business and management, which is by far the most popular degree awarded. She is now a bright 22-year-old ready to finally begin real life. She's been looking forward to this for as long as she can remember. Like most of her peers, she had to take out significant student loans, but she feels she did okay, since she researched the amount of debt most people her age graduated with and she is right in the middle of the pack with $37,172 owed. Luckily, right after graduation, she secured a position as a business analyst on an average salary. Six months later, when her loan payback period officially began, she was a full-fledged adult millennial.

But she almost had a mental breakdown when she received her repayment packet in the mail outlining her minimum monthly payment of $393. She was already struggling to afford her rent of $900/month, a car payment of $200/month, a car insurance payment of $125/month, utilities of $100/month, plus whatever she spent on food. How come no one taught her how to budget for all these things? And how in the world would she afford all these bills plus a $393/month student loan payment on an average starting salary?

The problem with pre-college debt analysis (if there is any) is that it typically doesn't factor in the cost of living after graduation. Kids at 18 decide what to study based on the average starting salaries majors are afforded upon graduation, then they deduce that they'll easily be able to pay off a $37,000 loan within a few years with a $50,000 to $60,000 starting salary. WRONG. The standard repayment timetable for federal loans is ten years. Because of the incomplete pre-college debt analysis, in fact it takes four-year degree holders an average of 19.7 years to repay their loans, according to a study by the OneWisconsin Institute. This is a huge problem and produces the same effect on loan interest as a mortgage does. According to a 2017 report conducted by New America, a nonprofit, nonpartisan think tank, the average student loan interest rate awarded in 2017 was 5.8%. That figure includes both federal and private loans. This means that even if Jessica paid off her loans in ten years, she would spend an extra $12,868 in interest alone, which makes for a total amount quite different than the $37,172 she was initially worried about. As research suggests, she likely won't pay them off for close to 20 years, so her total repayment amount would become $63,300, which equates to an extra $26,428 paid in interest over the 20-year period.

Unfortunately for Jessica, she is just now realizing the consequences of her actions. She is trying her hardest to enjoy her new job, but she just can't find the meaning in it. She enjoyed college, but she feels tricked for signing up for so much debt in exchange for a fancy piece of paper that forces her to go to work every day at a job she doesn't enjoy. Jessica is now a hostage to the system, just like 44.7 million other Americans. We've been corralled into a cycle that boils down to needing money for college, needing college for a job, then needing a job for money to pay for college. How ridiculous? I wish I could say I wasn't in the same sinking ship that Jessica boarded, but four years ago I found myself in an even more extreme financial situation. Before I describe my awakening to all this madness, it's necessary to fill you in on how I got there.

MY QUEST FOR HIGH ACHIEVEMENT

As you know, when I was heading into my senior year of high school, my family was experiencing life-changing financial difficulties. As a 17-year-old, my natural response to my situation was to work as hard as possible to get into the best university I could. My goal was large but simple: get into a prestigious university, acquire an elite degree, use it to get a six-figure job, and end my family's hardship forever. Therefore, my entire focus became my GPA, my SAT score, my extracurricular activities, and of course, my part-time job. Failure was out of the question. It's not that I wasn't already working extremely hard, but that last year and a half of high school I was downright concerned with becoming who I needed to be to get to the next step—an elite university.

As if it counts for anything now, even to this day I must acknowledge that I built an impressive resume for a high schooler. I graduated 15th in my class out of about 300; I was captain of the varsity football team my junior and senior year (with multiple all-district honors at my positions); I accumulated over 425 volunteer hours at various organizations; I was chosen to represent our entire school for what's called the Strategic Planning Committee; I had an SAT score over 2100; I was one of two who received the largest scholarship available ($8,000) from my city's education foundation; and I was given the Mr. McKinney North Award upon graduation, which is an award presented to a senior who most embodies what it means to be a Bulldog (our mascot) that the entire school faculty votes for. To my surprise, all of that was enough to get me accepted into the best school in Texas, and perhaps the most prestigious school in the south, Rice University. On top of that, they offered me a position on the football team, a division-1 program. I was beyond thrilled! My plan was working out perfectly. Little did I know that *prestige = rigor* and *division-1 = no free time*.

The next four years proved the hardest of my life up to that point. My days consisted of 5:00 a.m. wakeups for 6:00 a.m. weights, then straight to breakfast before my 8:00 a.m. class. I'd be in class until noon, then straight back to class after a quick lunch until 2:00 p.m. As soon as class was over, I'd rush over to the stadium for team meetings that started at 2:45 p.m. sharp. After meetings, we would practice for three hours. By the time practice was over, it'd be close to 7:00 p.m. Due to my engineering workload, two days a week I had some sort of lab that ran from 7 to 10 p.m., so oftentimes I'd have to leave practice early, ride my bike to dinner as fast as I could, then somehow get to lab on time. After practice or lab, depending on what day it was, I would attempt to do my homework assignments before my self-regulated mandatory bedtime at 1:00 a.m. Through trial and error, I found there was no way I could function on less than four hours of sleep. This experience led me to believe that I would never encounter anything more demanding, more stressful, more difficult, or more inhibiting.

For much of my college career, I found myself taking refuge in what my life would be like after graduation, when I finally had that six-figure job. In my mind, that's when I would show everyone who's boss. I was playing the long ball and practicing delayed gratification by sacrificing my college years in exchange for a professional salary upon graduation. I could've gone to any state school and had a blast like most people, but I chose to suffer so I could have my name on the fanciest piece of paper money could buy. The chip on my shoulder whispering in my ear the entire time, "No one will ever be able to take this away from me."

Just as I had planned and right on schedule, I graduated from Rice with a Bachelor of Science in Civil Engineering and a minor in Energy & Water Sustainability. We even got away with a conference championship and two bowl games, which I am forever grateful to have been a part of. Due to financial aid, I thought I got off the hook quite reasonably in terms of total debt, with a moderate $50,000, less than the cost of one year at Rice. I was fortunate enough to have two different internships during my time in college. This greatly increased my job options upon graduation. In fact, by the fall of my senior year, I had four solid job offers on the table. Three were in oil and gas in Houston, and one was in engineering and construction in Dallas. By everyone else's standards, I crushed it.

Finally, what I worked my whole life to achieve was becoming a reality. It was time to stop spending and start earning a full-time income. It was time to help support my family in a more meaningful way. Due to the price of oil and the unknown future of the oil and gas industry, I chose to return to Dallas and accepted the position in engineering and construction. I was immediately given a private office and everything I could've asked for to be successful. I was back to big-dog status.

Two years into my career, at 24, my goal had become reality. I was making six-figures, and I was in the top 1% of income-earners for my age. Just as I had planned, it was time to achieve the final piece of my goal—to end my family's hardship. The only problem was that I had no money to spare because I was spending all my income repaying my student loans and affording an average cost of living in Dallas. How can someone in my position not have any spare money? Consider this: due to my family's credit plunge caused by the Great Recession, the only loans we were approved for were unsubsidized "Parent-Plus" loans. These loans were the only way I was able to attend school in the first place. The problem? These loans began accruing interest as soon as they were issued—my first year. They also had interest rates of almost 9%! How is someone supposed to make any money to pay for these loans during school to stop an absurd interest rate from compounding out of control? The answer is—there is no way unless you have outside help. As you can imagine, my parents couldn't pay for them, so I spent my first two years out of college paying essentially nothing but interest on what was accruing while I was busting my butt in college. I spent two years just getting back to my original $50,000 balance, two years without progress. This was one of the most defeating realizations I've ever had, almost $15,000 in interest alone down the drain. To add to the drama, my initial minimum monthly payment was over $750. It's no wonder I wasn't making any financial progress.

On top of my new financial difficulties, I was experiencing stress, anxiety, and depression unlike ever before due to the job I had signed up for. I got to the point where I had to see a neurologist for help since I could not come to terms with the reality that I signed up for. I was so stressed and anxious that I was taking prescription sleeping pills in hopes to get some sleep at night, and Adderall by day to remain awake and energetic enough to perform my miserable 12 to 14 hours of work. I felt there was no way out because I needed my high income to pay for my student loans. I felt chained to my desk. Wasn't this supposed to be the best time in my life? Why did I just sacrifice eight years of my life practicing delayed gratification to be in this situation? I began to deliberate whether the system had duped me, or if I had duped myself. Either way, it was exactly the opposite of what I thought I was looking forward to before.

A PERFECTLY DESIGNED TRAP

At this point, I came to another incredibly sad realization—if I was in the top 1% of income earners and faring extremely poorly, this meant many of my peers were suffering also, probably worse than I was. This hit the empath in me hard. Intense suffering begins when someone realizes they are being forced against their will to go to work every day just to pay for the degree that got them there in the first place. The suffering increases when they realize they've sacrificed their youth because there is no way out until their debt is paid, and the suffering peaks when they realize they don't enjoy the career path they've chosen. Could it be that some entity has intentionally increased the cost of college so much knowing that it would pigeonhole millions of Americans into going to work every day? A quote from Fyodor Dostoyevsky points to this possibility: "The best way to keep a prisoner from escaping is to make sure he never knows he's in prison." It's no wonder the American economy has been strong in the second decade of the 2000s: an entire generation is being forced against their will to work full-time.

The curious thing about the investment in higher education is that there are no refunds, no transfers, and no possibility of escape through bankruptcy. If I invest in a car, I purchase the car with a loan from a third party for $20,000. Cars are depreciating assets that lose thousands of dollars in value just a few minutes after you leave the lot. Let's say I got myself into a bad situation and needed to get rid of the car. I have options. I can go back to the dealer and see if they'll take it back for a similar price. I can sell it to another dealership and hope for a loss of a few thousand, or I can sell it privately and hope for a smaller loss. I made an investment, it wasn't the right thing for me, and I want to get out of it, so I do. And I'm willing to pay the small price for a bad choice. The same concept applies to mortgages in the short-term, although this one is a bit tougher if I can't find a buyer, obviously. The important thing to realize is that I'd still have options to minimize my loss. This concept does not apply to the investment of higher education. Why is this? And how many people would be interested in getting out of their investment if it were possible? My guess is many. Probably around 1.5 trillion dollars worth.

We should be putting much more emphasis on our young people's decision to invest in higher education instead of continuing to apply the "one size fits all" mentality that everyone must go to college to be successful. There are so many other available life-paths that I've been exposed to from traveling so much. Americans live in a little bubble that is severely limiting our young people's knowledge of their life options. We must begin to change this ideology immediately. The health, fulfillment, and collective potential of our future generations depends on it.

One way to combat our current "one size fits all" ideology is by making it normal (and acceptable) to integrate a gap year between high-school and college. I highly recommend that more Americans begin taking at least six months to travel between high-school and beginning college or pursuing an alternative. This is proving remarkably successful among other developed nations such as Germany, Australia, and many Scandinavian countries for a variety of reasons. One notable reason is the people that do it are exposed to many other ways of living a happy and fulfilled life that they wouldn't have known about if they went directly to university. This massively increases their life options and helps them understand how they want to spend their lives before deciding to invest money and time. A gap year also enables people to better understand what they want to study if they decide college is ultimately the route they want to take. In my eyes, it's much better to spend $5,000 traveling for six months to find that you don't want to go to college rather than immediately enrolling because it's the "right thing to do" and wasting four years and tens of thousands of dollars just to realize you don't enjoy the career path you've chosen. Additionally, traveling for a year at 18 provides a global education in itself. People will better understand who they are, where they come from, what makes them unique, and what value they have to give to the world. This is arguably the greatest benefit a gap year affords. Lastly, this system produces an amazing sense of humility and maturity that is evident in the young people who are taking a gap year that I've met around the globe. I've been impressed with them, and I thoroughly enjoy getting to guide and direct young people trying to navigate the early stages of life.

THE FUTURE OF HIGHER EDUCATION IN AMERICA

To understand the future fate of America's higher education system, we must first analyze the projected future supply vs. demand. There is already a severe supply vs. demand imbalance, and because the future projections don't account for the absurdity of the return-on-investment myth, higher education as we know it will soon be a thing of the past. One of the most telling statistics available is from a 2016 PayScale study on underemployment. PayScale defines underemployment as "having part-time work but wanting to work full-time or, holding a job that doesn't require or utilize your education, experience or training." In the underemployment study of 900,000 Americans, they found that 76% of people are not using their education and 24% are working part-time but would like to be working full-time. This shows us that there is currently a massive higher education supply surplus: there are too many people with expensive pieces of paper and not enough roles and positions available for them to occupy, so they are settling for whatever job they can get in order to live and pay for their student loans. This should be among the primary pieces of information afforded to high schoolers trying to decide if they want to go to college or not. Why work so hard to get an expensive degree, go into a crazy amount of debt, and then most likely not be able to use it anyway?

Incorrectly, the projections available on the future demand for higher education are purely based on the number of high schoolers that will graduate each year in America. This hasn't been an issue in previous decades, since the college-going rate in America has been increasing even as high school enrollments plateaued. Because of this, colleges base their financial calculations on the present college-going rate, which is just south of 70% of high school graduates. Even if we accepted this erroneous method of demand projection, the future demand for higher education is due to decrease substantially in the next ten years. According to *The Washington Post*, the number of high school graduates is projected to remain relatively flat for the next several years, but between 2026 and 2031, the ranks of high school graduates are expected to drop by 9%. Even so, these declining demand projections don't account for the percentage of high school graduates proceeding to college decreasing. I believe the college-going rate will soon begin to decline as our young people finally realize the following:

- The impacts of accepting student loan debt.
- The low likelihood of using their expensive degree.
- The 19.7-year average payback period that consequently yields colossal interest payments.
- The alternative to traditional college in favor of a new, much less expensive technology for educating students: online learning.
- The possibility of earning substantial income online without the need for a college degree.

In the coming decades, this decline in demand will lead to many colleges and universities across the country closing their doors because they will not have the enrollment funds to continue paying their enormous overheads.

MY LIFE NUMBERS ... YIKES!

Another year into my career, I was doing my best to accept the ideology that gets most people through—work is supposed to be difficult; that's why it's called work. Again, I found myself taking refuge in the "next stage" and started looking long term. I projected how long it would take me to pay off my student loan debt, given a few strategic raises over the next 10 to 20 years. I even projected my future spending, assuming I would be blessed with a wife and kids. Additionally, I added retirement savings and a few other key factors that enabled me to get an idea of what I was working towards. The numbers were saddening to say the least. I saw that if I continued what I was doing, I would end up working for the rest of my life, despite my relatively high level of income. This was step one in realizing I needed a lifestyle redesign.

Like most other suburban American kids raised in the last 25 years, my options were: go to college, go to college, or go to college. It wasn't that I wouldn't have been allowed to go a different route, it's just that I wasn't really given any more appealing options at 18. Because of my radical lifestyle redesign, I now get asked if I regret going to college and taking out student loans to do so, since I'm seemingly not using my engineering degree. My answer is simply that I don't live my life with regrets because I know that I chose the best option based on whatever information I had during decision time. Looking back on my choices, I'm proud of the path that I took given the information that I had. But what they're really asking is not if I regret my decision to go to college, but if I could go back, what would I do differently? If I could somehow travel back in time and get another shot at being 18, knowing what I know today, I'd procure a small business loan for as much as

I could and get on my way. At least if I squandered it somehow, it could be forgiven, unlike the $65,000 lifetime risk of college debt that is unforgivable by declaration.

Today, my entire lifestyle has been reverse engineered to my satisfaction. I'm utilizing the problem-solving abilities I gained obtaining a prestigious engineering degree and applying them to life design. I developed a decision-making system that is both qualitative and quantitative to help me understand my choices qualitatively, financially, and meaningfully. In this way, I can express gratitude towards my college degree and continue to build on the positives. Building on the gratitude, I can say with certainty that my story and my proposed solutions wouldn't hold as much weight had I not gone the traditional route first and excelled at it. I would also not possess the drive to tackle this problem head-on had I not experienced the pain intimately for myself first.

As I mentioned previously, innovation always crushes cultural conditioning one way or another. As you'll find in Part II (Multiple Passive Income Streams) and Part III (Tiny Living), I've created two innovative ways for people to escape the societal traps of mortgages and student loans. Both parts offer a different solution to attaining financial freedom as quickly as possible. Before we get into them, it's necessary to revisit the concept of retirement. As you'll see, the typical way of life as it pertains to retirement in America drastically needs to be innovated. Our ability to live our lives to our fullest potential demands it.

CHAPTER 5

Retirement Revisited

PEOPLE ARE STRANGE: THEY ARE
CONSTANTLY ANGERED BY TRIVIAL THINGS,
BUT ON A MAJOR MATTER LIKE TOTALLY
WASTING THEIR LIVES, THEY HARDLY SEEM
TO NOTICE.

Charles Bukowski

Tradition tells us that we must work most of our lives to save enough money to enable ourselves to quit working and then fund our lives from our accumulated savings. For some reason, the age society has chosen as the sweet spot for quitting work is 65. This life path is as widely accepted as the idea that one needs a college degree to be successful. In short, retiring at 65 is the goal that most Americans are working towards. Everyone knows this, but few stop to think about the consequences of this path.

Most people are only analyzing their life choices *qualitatively*, meaning they are making decisions based on feelings alone. My goal is to show you a way to judge your life choices *quantitatively*, in addition to your existing qualitative methods. This means understanding the numbers associated with your life choices and using them to make more informed decisions. Using quantitative data allows us to understand what financial goals we are working towards, and if/when we will reach them. Analyzing our lives in this way gives us important insight into the future by giving us the information we need in the present to weigh our choices against the sacrifices associated with them.

American financial experts advise that the average 65-year-old should have between $1 million and $1.5 million set aside for retirement. Since 80 years is the average life expectancy for both males and females in America in 2020, this amount, on average, would ensure that someone would make it to their death at 80 without having to make any more money. So how many of us are accomplishing our retirement goals by choosing the traditional route? How many of us can retire at 65 with $1 million in the bank? The first thing you need to know is that the average American has nothing saved for retirement. *Nothing.* According to data from the Federal Reserve's Survey of Consumer Finances, the most common account balance for a retirement account is exactly zero dollars. Furthermore, a 2018 study conducted by Northwestern Mutual found that over one-third of baby boomers currently in or approaching retirement have between $0 and $25,000 set aside. Because of this collective lack of savings, traditional retirement is quickly approaching a major crisis that is not receiving the attention it should. In the coming decades, millions of Americans will get too old to continue working without the means to stop. Millennials, crippled by debt from graduation, will turn this crisis into a full-blown catastrophe in about 30 years. Additionally, Social Security, designed to prevent exactly this problem, covers less than half of an average retiree's cost of living at this point, and that will decrease further as the crisis develops. So how did we get into this mess? And why are the financial results of lifelong full-time work overwhelmingly negative? The answer to both questions is the same: people don't know their life numbers in a flawed system.

CLOCK OF LIFE

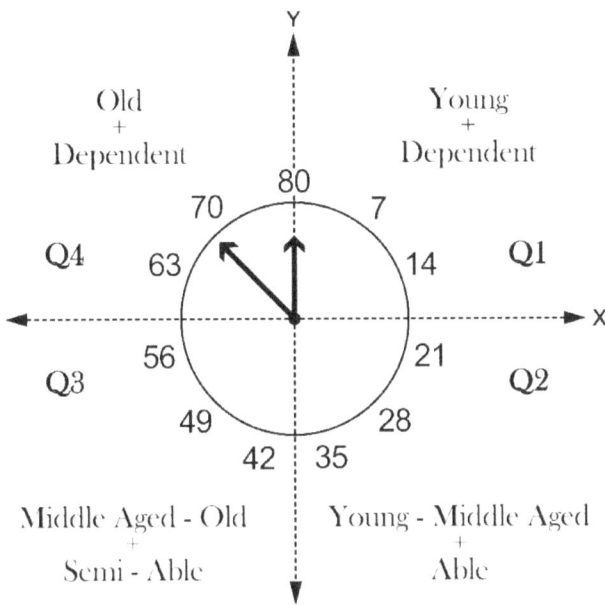

For my visual learners, I've illustrated our brief time on earth as what I call "The Clock of Life," as you can see above. This is a visual aid to help you begin using quantitative analysis to drive your life choices. It's designed to show you a glimpse of your life cycle—to shock you into life wherever you fall on the clock. It's meant to help you visualize the fact that your time is not only limited but also that your "best" time is fleeting. The Clock of Life illustrates this is your only life—your one shot, and you don't get a redo. As you can see, the clock ends at age 80, the current life expectancy of the average American; not a guarantee but a helpful benchmark that will guide you to the light. Living over 80 is becoming more common and should be viewed as a bonus.

An important aspect to grasp about the Clock is that there are the four quadrants.

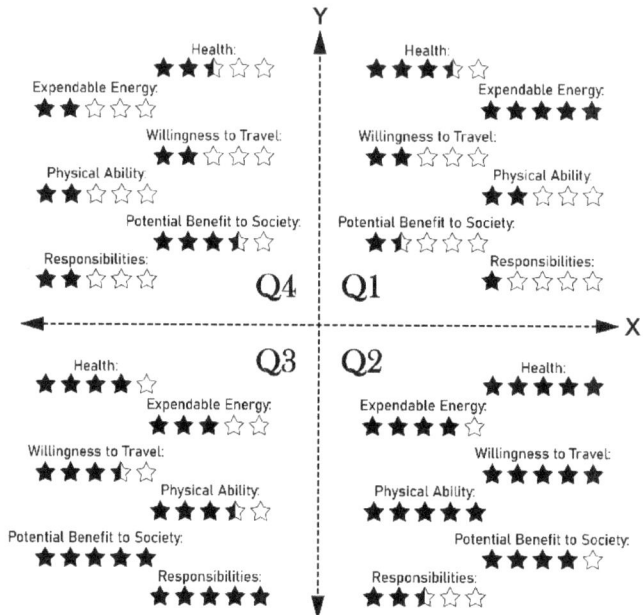

In quadrant 1 (Q1), we are in literal and relative infancy, dependent on a caretaker to provide our basic needs, such as food, shelter, and clothing. We have an amazing amount of expendable energy, but we don't know how to harness it yet. Responsibilities are at an all-time low, and we are just beginning to understand who we are and what value we have to give. In quadrant 2 (Q2), we are young to middle-aged and in our physical prime. This is the sweet spot for physical ability, health, willingness to travel, expendable energy, and responsibilities. Quantitatively speaking, in this quadrant we possess the greatest potential to enjoy the amazing things our world has to offer with willingness to travel at an all-time high. In quadrant 3 (Q3), we are middle-aged to old and begin to really feel the impacts of gravity. Our physical abilities aren't what they used to be, and our expendable energy is on the decline. We are still generally healthy and free to travel, but we have gained many responsibilities that keep us mostly stationary. Here, our potential benefit to society is at an all-time high. In quadrant 4 (Q4) we are getting old and at the end of our life. Our physical abilities have largely escaped us, we lack the energy to perform basic tasks, and we are riddled with health problems and therefore not willing to travel as much, if any. Like Q1, we are again dependent on a caretaker to provide our basic needs.

Life is about the journey to reaching your personal potential, and you must give yourself a fighting chance to get there. How do you give yourself a chance? You emphasize being rich in time in Q2 and Q3 relative to Q4. This means understanding that your physical potential between the ages of 20 and 60 is at its optimum and designing your life accordingly. It means taking advantage of being young and able before it's too late. It means giving yourself the gift of time in Q2 and Q3 instead of in Q4. Following this logic, our individual potential is greatest in Q2 and Q3 because we are in our physical prime—after all, we live in a physical world. Accordingly, there is no point slaving away in these quadrants just so we can finally gain financial freedom (become time-rich) in Q4. In fact, by waiting to become time-rich until Q4, we are effectively wasting our years with our greatest potential. By that time, our physical abilities, expendable energy, health, and willingness to travel are all relatively poor; meaning our focus is likely to be on our poor health and lack of energy rather than using our gifts to reach our potential. If you gain financial freedom for the first time at age 65, you will realize almost instantaneously that your options are extremely limited. If you don't believe me, just go volunteer at your local nursing home for a day and see for yourself what you're working towards within the traditional system. Ask the residents what they're looking forward to, how they feel today, and if they have any regrets in life. I should say that I do know people in Q4 that are still highly active, healthy, and love to travel, but they are by no means the norm.

IGNORANCE IS NOT BLISS

Most people, especially millennials, are loosely working towards a retirement goal, not knowing their life numbers. They don't know when they'll be able to retire or how much money they must set aside to do so. Furthermore, it's difficult to project what our future situation is going to be, so we simplify the goal to that magical number of 65 and put our heads down to go back to work. If you don't know your life numbers (when you'll achieve financial freedom), I challenge you to learn them as soon as possible. Knowing your numbers can be extremely empowering. You might be surprised when you establish your financial plan taking all the recommended steps because it forces you to realize your goal. Once you realize your goal and you can see what it's going to require to get there, you can judge whether the sacrifice required is worth it or not. To help you understand your own life numbers, I've created a free tool to help get you started. By no means is the tool all encompassing, but it'll give you a snapshot of where you are currently and lead you to begin analyzing your life more quantitatively. How to access this tool will be included at the end of this chapter.

To further illustrate the point that you might unknowingly be making a huge sacrifice you are not okay with, allow me to walk you through an exercise that changed the way I think about my current life. Before we begin, know that I'm advocating for financial freedom at any age so that people can engage in meaningful work instead of forced meaningless work. To begin the exercise, recognize that your current goal is to live a comfortable life and save enough money by the time you're 65 so that you can stop working forever and begin doing the things you actually want to do. Regardless of your age, fast forward in your mind to being 65 years old. Here you are, still working every day. But good news! Today is the day you've been waiting 43 years for—the day you finally get to retire. You just had your retirement party at the office. You did it! Now what? You probably need a nap; you're old!

Look at you, you did everything right. You worked hard, you're out of debt, you own a house, and you saved plenty for retirement. You might even get lucky and have a little splurge cash from our good friends over at Social Security. Now answer three questions for me (apply your experience in the working world thus far):

1. What might you be thinking on that day?
   - Maybe relieved it's finally over? Grateful for the opportunity? Ready to go home? I saw myself full of regret for not giving myself the time necessary to serve my own purpose and become who I know deep down I can be.
2. Would you say your working life has been an enjoyable experience?
   - If the answer is currently no, maybe you think you'll find a better job and be happy by the time you hit retirement. At least that's the song I was singing for a while. It's possible, but unlikely without lifestyle redesign.
3. Have you made a positive difference in other people's lives? (Was your work meaningful?)
   - This was a breakthrough question for me. Your work MUST be meaningful to YOU or you're wasting your time.

My answers to these three questions caused me to re-evaluate my life choices and realize it was time to start betting on myself.

What if there was another way to approach retirement, would you entertain the possibility of a different way? A way that could save you from doing something you don't get excited about for 43 years of your life? I must warn you; this new approach isn't for everyone. It's not for people who find their self-worth in material things, it's not for people who aren't willing to do whatever it takes, and it's surely not for people who value money more than their time. I hope you're seeing the trend here. Time is our most important asset, and it's crucial to look at our years both qualitatively and quantitatively.

Conventionally, retirement and financial freedom mean the same thing, but today there's a catch: you don't have to be retired to be financially free. This is an extremely important thing to realize. Again, I am not advocating for early retirement so that people stop working and do nothing. I'm advocating for financial freedom at any age so that people can engage in meaningful work instead of being forced to sacrifice their lives for money.

CASH FLOW & FINANCIAL FREEDOM

In today's world, anyone can become financially free with a little tool called cash flow. This method works if you're 17, 27, 47, or 97, and you don't need $1 million in savings. Cash flow is the difference between old people who are financially free and young people who are financially free. Likewise, another difference between old people who are time-rich and young people who are time-rich is the total amount of cash reserves each one has. They are likely living on similar amounts of cash per month, meaning their spending is in the same ballpark. But the old people are withdrawing their money from retirement accounts and the young people have income streams that are funding their lifestyles and enabling them to do meaningful things. The average young person with financial freedom still has a cost of living, but the money is not coming from a large stash they have accumulated by blood, sweat, and tears over the course of 43-plus years. It's likely coming from digital business ventures that they were smart enough to set up.

It is possible to design online businesses around your desired lifestyle. As a matter of fact, it's easier to do it this way. This is exactly what I did for the entirety of 2019. My version of the American Dream was to travel full-time and photograph parts of the world I was interested in, which included Hawaii, Australia, New Zealand, Fiji, Indonesia, Singapore, Italy, and Spain. I created a spreadsheet, calculated every single dime necessary to make it a reality (with a 15% margin of error), and figured out that I needed approximately $2,200 per month for the first 2.5 months, then about $1,000 per month after that. I was shocked that my idea of an extraordinary life would cost me less than it would've cost me to stay in my Dallas apartment for the year. Fortunately for me, I was already producing passive income online selling private-label products on Amazon. I just needed to scale up my current operations and add one more source of income to allow for some savings. Whether you choose to stick with the traditional path, go all-in on passive income ventures, or a mix of both, it's still extremely important to save for the future. Undoubtedly, we all eventually need savings for things like healthcare and assisted living or caretaking. This is accomplished in the same way regardless of your lifestyle choices—a portion of your income is set aside for future needs.

The beautiful thing about the variety of digital venture models available is that you can create ventures (streams of income) that are specifically allocated to certain expenses, both present and future. You can create one source of income for your current cost of living, one source of income for savings, another for your student debt, another for your mortgage, and so on. Once they're setup and optimized, by design, each venture generally requires around two to three hours of work per week. This is all possible due to the efficiencies that the internet has created and the amazing and inexpensive tools that everyone now has at their disposal. You might have a hard time believing this is possible without knowing the first thing about creating an online business, but I'll walk you through exactly what to do in Part II—Multiple Passive Income Streams.

We are living in a time with unparalleled comforts and resources at our disposal. What legitimate concerns do we have compared to previous generations? Financial worries are stressful, don't get me wrong. But they don't compare to issues our ancestors faced. Sleepless nights caused by financial stress don't have anything on sleepless nights caused by lack of food, lack of shelter, lack of clothing, and so on. What issues do you have today that financial freedom can't solve? Probably not many, if any. In the last 15 years alone, our society has made some of the greatest technological advancements the world has ever known, and you are fortunate to be able to use them for personal gain and prosperity. The world has changed in the blink of an eye. There is a global revolution underway though it is only just beginning. We are all part of it as either a creator or a consumer. In the following chapter, I'll explain the details of the Digital Revolution and show you how to change your mind and habits so that you can turn your value into digital value and join the new rich—people rich in free-time and liberty.

To access the free tool that enables you to learn your life numbers, visit **www.777tribe.com/life-numbers.**

PART II

Multiple Passive Income Streams

CHAPTER 6

The Digital Revolution

EVERYONE YOU MEET ALWAYS ASKS IF YOU HAVE A CAREER, ARE MARRIED, OR OWN A HOUSE, AS IF LIFE IS SOME SORT OF GROCERY LIST. BUT NO ONE EVER ASKS YOU IF YOU ARE HAPPY.

Heath Ledger

To deeply appreciate the tools modern humanity currently has at our disposal, it is necessary to understand where we came from and how our species has evolved over the last 200,000 years. Many people don't know (or prefer not to recognize) that our specific breed of human, *Homo sapiens*, first came to be around 200,000 years ago in Eastern Africa. At that time, there were many other species of human beings that, like us, first evolved from chimpanzees about 2.5 million years prior, according to Richard Klein—author of *The Human Career*, which chronicles the evolution of people from the earliest primates. More precisely stated by Klein, both chimpanzees (*Pan troglodytes* and *Pan paniscus*) and various hominins, including the genus *Homo*, evolved from a common ancestor. Now, let me just say that I believe creationism and evolutionism are not mutually exclusive and believing in one or the other is a limiting point of view. Regardless of your personal beliefs, the goal of this chapter is to reshape your understanding of where you fall in human history so that you can begin to appreciate and take full advantage of what is available to you as a *Homo sapiens* living in the twenty first century.

Accordingly, there have been five major human revolutions since our species' first appearance. Each revolution fundamentally changed our way of life and enabled us to rapidly evolve and scale our total population. We can think of the following revolutions as the major inflection points of human history:

- The Cognitive Revolution (70,000 years ago)
  - 1,000—10,000 *Homo sapiens* living
- The Agricultural Revolution (12,000 years ago)
  - 4 million *Homo sapiens* living
- The Writing and Numbers Revolution (5,000 years ago)
  - 14 million *Homo sapiens* living
- The Scientific Revolution (500 years ago)
  - 500 million *Homo sapiens* living
- The Industrial Revolution (200 years ago)
  - 1 billion *Homo sapiens* living

As you'll see shortly, we are collectively entering into a sixth major global revolution—The Digital Revolution.

Before we briefly delve into the five historic human revolutions for an idea of what they were and how they changed humanity's way of life, we must first look at the definition of evolutionary success. In another fantastic account of human history titled *Sapiens: A Brief History of Humankind*, Yuval Noah Harari defines the currency of evolution as "neither hunger nor pain, but rather copies of DNA helixes. Just as the economic success of a company is measured only by the number of dollars in its bank account, not by the happiness of its employees, so the evolutionary success of a species is measured by the number of copies of its DNA." Nonetheless, the sole measure of humanity's evolutionary success is the number of people in existence. By this definition, from one revolution to the next, we experienced unparalleled evolutionary success. But what the definition of evolutionary success doesn't account for is the collective quality of life and the level of individual suffering that exists within a population. As we dive into each revolution, you'll see how each one brought new capabilities and efficiencies that enabled us to increase our population's size, but largely produced more problems than we had to begin with.

THE COGNITIVE REVOLUTION

The Cognitive Revolution can be thought of as the emergence of language beyond basic grunts and hand gestures, and the first time we could transmit large quantities of information, both factual and nonfactual (i.e., non-literal language). It is important to note that humans have lived as hunter-gatherers for the vast majority of our existence. According to Harari, it wasn't until we began to organize the use of plants and animals around 12,000 years ago that we began to make the shift from nomads to planned cities. Some evolutionary psychologists claim that several of our modern-day social and psychological ideals were shaped during this long pre-agricultural era. Since we spent close to 200,000 years working together in small tribes to satisfy our basic needs, and only the last 12,000 years living in a domesticated environment, from an evolutionary perspective, it is argued that our species hasn't had the time to completely adapt to our new way of life.

Because of this, it's possible that a part of us still subconsciously inhabits the same nomadic world of 12,000 years ago. This has interesting impacts on modern society, but it would take a separate book to explain them properly. In short, we could be compared to ancient beasts doing our best to navigate public transportation, corporate America, taxes, and nuclear family life, while trying to convince ourselves that we are evolved, modern, and sophisticated. Thankfully for us, the Cognitive Revolution brought with it a new human ability: to imagine, communicate, and create better paths forward. This is very important, because while some of our engrained habits might be counterproductive in modern culture, we have been able to retain our most important asset—the power to innovate. Even if our DNA hasn't had the time to completely adapt to our new way of life, our adaptive minds have been able to make up for any evolutionary shortcomings.

THE AGRICULTURAL REVOLUTION

As stated in *Sapiens*, the Agricultural Revolution began 58,000 years after the Cognitive Revolution. This revolution brings us to only 12,000 years ago. I find it hard to believe that it took us so long to begin using plants and animals to our advantage, but when you look at the impacts this revolution had on our collective well-being, things begin to make more sense. Like some of the other major global human revolutions, the essence of the Agricultural Revolution was the ability to keep more people alive under worse conditions. At this point we began establishing permanent villages strategically located in fertile lands and near water supplies. This enabled the population to grow at rates never before seen on earth. Women could have a baby each year and wean the child at an earlier age. Thank goodness, because the extra hands were necessary in the fields. Unfortunately, the extra mouths quickly decimated the food supplies, so even more crops had to be planted to support the growing population. Diseases became more prevalent due to the amount of people and animals interacting regularly in small areas, and children competed with one another for food. Because of this, child mortality rates soared, and one in three children died before reaching age twenty, yet the population continued to increase because births still outpaced deaths.

It's important to note that this was also the beginning of worry associated with future economic security. Today, we know this as stress. Farmers began to worry because they could finally do something about their future. Harari states that "farmers could plow another field, excavate another irrigation canal and plant more crops, all while putting off until winter or the following year the eating of the food they craved today." So why would we have chosen to proceed with this revolution in the first place? That's the curious thing about these revolutions—no one could possibly foresee the impacts of their innovations. It took generations to transform society and, by then, no one remembered that we had ever lived differently. Additionally, population growth led humanity past the point of no return. There were too many mouths to feed to go back to our old hunting-and-gathering lifestyle.

THE WRITING & NUMBERS REVOLUTION

For thousands of years after the Agricultural Revolution, human societies remained relatively small and simple. In fact, Harari states that it took us another 7,000 years to get to the point where we realized we needed a way of storing and documenting information outside of our brains so we could scale further. We concluded that to manage large amounts of people successfully, we needed a way to collect mathematical data about people's incomes, possessions, debts, property, and more. It was not enough to legislate and tell stories about the gods; empires needed to collect taxes to make our larger societies work properly. This was the beginning of writing and numbers. Without the invention of writing and numbers, humanity would likely still be living in the age immediately following the Agricultural Revolution. These tools allowed us to collectively organize beyond our wildest dreams and enabled us to scale our population from approximately 14 million to 500 million in less than 5,000 years. While this revolution produced many more capabilities than we had previously, the most important thing is the scale that it enabled us to reach. It was the rise of empires and religions, art and philosophy, and math and reading, among other things. This revolution made life infinitely more complicated but also gave us a new world of possibilities to enjoy.

THE SCIENTIFIC REVOLUTION

About 4,500 years after the beginning of writing and numbers came the Scientific Revolution. Descartes, Bacon, Hobbes, Galileo, and Newton have become the founding fathers of the Scientific Revolution. They discovered a world that appeared to offer secrets of itself that were never before seen. These secrets showed themselves mainly through quantifiable statements. This led them to believe that the natural world was designed in a rationally ordered way and it was the job of human beings to understand the layout of that order. The major negative effect that this revolution had on civilization was the unfortunate disjunct it created between human consciousness and the natural world. The scientific findings of this revolution brought us to the conclusion that the natural world has no spirit, no life of its own; it is defined by its mechanical processes; it is able to be completely understood by rational analysis; and it exists separately, independently from our participation in it. A further problem arises when we see that the scientific model is itself a development of human consciousness. The scientific model disregards myth and metaphor while purporting itself to be the only means to objective truth, but the scientific model itself is not necessarily objectively true, but yet only another myth, another structure by which the world may be experienced.

THE INDUSTRIAL REVOLUTION

The final major revolution was the Industrial Revolution, which occurred just 300 years after the Scientific Revolution. Note how the frequency of major revolutions has increased over time but still had similar impacts on our collective well-being and total population. The Industrial Revolution created new ways to convert energy and produce goods, which resulted in an explosion of human productivity. With our new tools, we cut down forests, drained swamps, dammed rivers, flooded plains, installed many miles of railroad tracks, and built booming metropolises. We destroyed habitats and many species of animals along the way as we molded the world to fit our new needs. We quickly turned our once blue and green planet into a concrete jungle of malls, agricultural use, and suburbs. Additionally, over the course of the last 200 years, industrial production methods have become standard in the agricultural industry. Because of this, farm animals stopped being viewed as living beings that could feel pain and distress and began to be treated as machines. Today, these animals are often mass-produced in factories where the length and quality of their existence depends solely on the profits of businesses. This is surely a negative impact of the Industrial Revolution. There is another monumental negative impact produced by this revolution that is also worth mentioning, which is how the assembly line schedule has become the template for almost all human activities.

In Chapter 18 of *Sapiens*, Harari provides a wonderful example to illustrate how humanity has created a love affair with clocks:

In contrast to medieval peasants and shoemakers, modern industry cares little about the sun or the season. It sanctifies precision and uniformity. For example, in a medieval workshop each shoemaker made an entire shoe, from sole to buckle. If one shoemaker was late for work, it did not stall the others. However, in a modern footwear-factory assembly line, every worker mans a machine that produces just a small part of a shoe, which is then passed on to the next machine. If the worker who operates machine no. 5 has overslept, it stalls all the other machines. In order to prevent such calamities, everybody must adhere to a precise timetable. Each worker arrives at work at the same time. Everybody takes their lunch break together and everybody goes home when a whistle announces that the shift is over—not when they have finished their project.

Because of this change, the typical modern person rushes from one thing to the next, looking at the clock several dozens of times per day to ensure they are on time. This is a far cry from the less rigid way of living our pre-Industrial Revolution ancestors enjoyed. Furthermore, the amount of stuff we began to produce had profound impacts on our way of life. It's even played a large part in creating a new widely accepted ethic—consumerism. For the first time in history, supply began to outweigh demand, creating an entirely new issue: how do we sell all this stuff and who is going to buy it?

THE DIGITAL REVOLUTION IS HERE!

The Digital Revolution has quickly turned consumerism upside down by connecting sellers with buyers all over the globe directly. The surplus of consumer goods combined with the capabilities of the internet has led to a historic increase in global production and distribution, but we're only just getting started. In human life terms, the internet is a teenager at best. It was only 20 years ago that people were still asking, "What is the internet and why would I need it?" Today, we can't live without it. Imagine what would happen if the internet suddenly crashed. Instantaneously, everyone you know would have exactly zero dollars and have no idea what to do with their time. Thankfully, there are no signs of anything but internet prosperity, although only half of the world's population currently has access to it. Furthermore, we're willing to completely rely on the internet for money management, but most people don't realize the earning potential at their fingertips.

It's amazing how quickly we've adopted this new technology and integrated it into our way of life. You can go pretty much anywhere in the world and find most of the population glued to their phones—Asia, America, Europe, South America, Australia, everywhere. Everyone is already addicted to the internet and the constant connectivity that if affords. Not surprisingly, we collectively take this amazing tool for granted. Most of us use it exclusively for entertainment, comparison on social media, and email at work. Everyone must know this, but few take advantage of the opportunities that this new culture produces for people that are willing to change their habits.

Just as we've only been able to write for 2.5% of our species' existence, we've only had the greatest tool humanity has ever known (the internet) for 0.0001% of our existence. We're at the forefront of the greatest technological revolution in the history of humankind! But instead of capitalizing on the opportunity and solving our individual problems, we'd rather endlessly scroll Instagram and binge-watch Netflix because it's much easier than the work required to reach our potential. Furthermore, just like the people who personally benefited from previous revolutions, the people who are benefiting from the Digital Revolution comprehend the historical significance of this new technology and are actively taking advantage of it. How? They are focused on creating rather than consuming.

LIFE-CHANGING LEVERAGE

Indeed, a new kind of value is being produced, a type of value we haven't seen before. Just as we've come to know that social capital is real, people are beginning to understand the value of digital capital. Amazingly, there are already thousands of ways to create digital capital and extract it in dollar form. Perhaps the most amazing thing about the internet, that most people don't realize yet, is the fact that it allows us to leverage our most important asset—our time. My life began to change the second I realized this. I'll never forget that moment.

I was still working in engineering and construction and sitting on my 20th 6:00 a.m. flight from Dallas to New York City in a short period of time. Each one of these flights required a 3:30 a.m. wake-up call. To make matters worse, the multi-million project I was traveling to was straight from hell, and I was apparently the only person responsible for it. I was sitting on the plane at 5:30 a.m., stressed, upset, and exhausted, knowing what I had to look forward to later that morning. Out of sheer desperation and frustration, the still, small voice inside me whispered, "There has to be a better way to make money than this." I was fed up, and my soul was beginning to speak up.

That was the first time I googled "how to make money online." It officially marked the beginning of my own Digital Revolution. As I started to understand the possibilities and saw that other people were successfully making money online, I became a sponge. I told myself, "If other people are doing this, I can too." I started consuming every piece of information I could find on the subject, from digital advertising to what types of businesses I could create. After a few months of learning, I decided to invest a few thousand dollars into taking a professional digital advertising course. I quickly became an expert at Facebook ads, Instagram ads, and Google advertising. These skills provided the foundation I needed to create, operate, and scale the five types of online businesses you'll learn about in Chapter 8. The most important thing to realize about paid digital advertising is what's called the return on ad spend (ROAS). The ROAS boils down to a return on investment and allows me to turn money into more money through Facebook and Google. My training taught me how to take $1 and turn it into $2, then take that $2 and turn it into $4, and so on. It also works with thousands of dollars. And sometimes, results are even better than that, depending on the product or service being advertised.

The premise for most of my online businesses is simple. Instead of being another zombie walking around aimlessly glued to my phone, I realized that through my new skills, I could reach anyone, anywhere, at any time, with just the right offer. You can think of paid digital advertising like a big beautiful (cheap) billboard strategically placed on a crowded highway with only your target audience traveling down it. The opportunities are virtually endless—there are 4.5 billion people online.

OUR COLLECTIVE NEXT STEP

My journey from rat race to freedom has led me to believe that widespread financial freedom is the next step in human evolution. I can't argue that this is hard to fathom, considering we have been collectively worried about our future economic prosperity since our first days of farming. But if there is any tool that can produce such an outcome, it's the internet, and the revolution is here. The internet has the capacity to free millions of people from unnecessarily busy lives. This would give people the time they need to quit rushing around while life passes them by and begin focusing on the things that matter most to them. Take this book, for example. I went to school thinking I wanted to be an engineer, yet when I chose liberty through passive income and tiny living, I discovered a whole new part of myself that is passionate about writing and providing the world with solutions to the problems I've personally experienced. And here you are reading my book! It's actually crazy how gaining liberty works, but it's hard to understand until you've experienced it for yourself. Just as the Declaration of Independence formalized America's revolution against Great Britain, you could consider this chapter the formalizing of my own digital revolution against the old world and a life without true liberty.

The essence of the Digital Revolution is the tools that allow us to leverage our time instead of trading our time for money. I've said it before, and I'll say it again: we are the luckiest people ever to walk the face of the earth. With widespread financial freedom achieved through the internet, we can potentially right the wrongs of each major revolution we've experienced. We can combine the greatest aspects of each period and pave a new way forward in the process. Fulfillment levels would be greater than they were in hunter-gatherer times; our collective health would be infinitely better than it was after the Agricultural Revolution; world peace would be well within our grasp, compared to the last 5,000 years; and we would be able to eliminate the need to constantly rush, which we've developed since the Industrial Revolution. This is what we've been waiting for! Now that I've established some of the possibilities of the Digital Revolution, in the next chapter we'll take a look at how passive income can impact our lives.

CHAPTER 7

The Impacts of Passive Income on Debt

IT'S NOT MORE VACATION WE
NEED—IT'S MORE VOCATION.

Eleanor Roosevelt

---⭐

P assive income is a godsend, but it's only achievable through the tools that the internet has enabled us to create. Passive income can be thought of as money consistently sent to your bank account without the need for your constant attention or large amounts of ongoing work. To clarify, each of the five income types you'll learn about in the next chapter are only considered passive because I've designed them that way. They are all legitimate businesses, but I've utilized one of my best attributes (resourcefulness) to make them passive in nature. Some of them are more passive than others, and they each have their positives and negatives with regard to the ongoing effort required.

Utilizing the tools and resources available to everyone on the internet, I've developed processes to create and manage multiple businesses without the need for help from anyone. In other words, I can create, manage, and scale them by myself from anywhere in the world with a sufficient Wi-Fi connection. Each business takes considerable time and effort to set up on the front end, but once they're running successfully, I usually expect about two or three hours of work per week per business venture, if that. Additionally, once they're running successfully, I have the option of outsourcing the weekly tasks to my virtual assistant. This effectively makes each business entirely passive, so I can focus on other things while still maintaining a consistent income. What a time to be alive!

As I'm sure you know, debt comes in all shapes and sizes. I've already addressed the two largest sources of household debt that exist in America (mortgages and student loans), but it's important to recognize the other two major debt culprits that are preventing millions of people from living their version of the American Dream: credit cards and auto loans. According to debt.org, in the second quarter of 2019, outstanding household debt increased dramatically for the 20th straight quarter, approaching a total balance of $14 trillion. Note that this is $1.2 trillion above the previous record high of $12.7 trillion, which occurred in the third quarter of 2008. I'm no economist, but we all saw what happened last time household debt reached these kinds of levels. This is an obvious issue that needs to be addressed quickly or we will surely end up in the same boat we put ourselves in previously in 2008 … it's only a matter of time.

As monstrous as this issue is, I believe I can do something about it. Allow me to demonstrate the power of passive income by returning to the lives of Jessica and Michael. For the purpose of these examples, we're going to assume that both Jessica and Michael invest in themselves, learn how to create income online, and begin producing an average of $500 per month in profit within six months of beginning their respective Digital Revolutions. As you'll see in the next chapter, $500 per month is quite conservative, considering the potential of my five venture options. After all, $500 per month equates to only $17 per day. Knowing what you know about the internet already, wouldn't you think you could find a way to make an extra $17 per day online?

THE POWER OF PASSIVE INCOME

Let's start with Jessica. Remember, Jessica starts with an initial student debt amount of $37,172. Based on recent statistics, she will be paying the minimum monthly payment for the next 19.7 years, which equates to a total amount paid of $63,300. As we learned in Chapter 4, this equates to $26,428 in interest alone over the 19.7-year period. Instead of accepting this as her fate, Jessica now has a way out. She can decide to leverage the efficiencies of the internet by creating additional income to drastically reduce her payback period and amount of interest paid. Applying her new $500 in profit per month, in addition to her minimum monthly payment, will reduce her payoff time to just six years instead of the 19.7 years she signed up for without realizing. (Six years of debt is more in line with what she thought she was getting herself into by accepting student loan debt initially.) Also, by taking this approach, she will save $18,445 in interest, compared to the traditional route. It doesn't stop there; instead of being $63,300 in the hole after 19.7 years, she will have an additional $81,623 from her $500 monthly profit over 14 years that would go into her savings account for 14 years, rather than towards her student debt. After six years, assuming she didn't accumulate any new debts, Jessica would be debt-free and able to claim a life of liberty for herself at only 28 years old, rather than 42 years old. She would then have a shot of fully enjoying life in Q2 and Q3 of her Clock of Life. Who knows, she just might change the world. This is the power of a relatively small stream of passive income!

Onward to Michael. Recall that Michael is three years into his first mortgage that had a starting balance of $309,200. Like most Americans, he was planning on paying his minimum monthly payment of $1,508 for the next 27 years, but due to his ludicrous work-life balance (or lack thereof) and a shortage of fulfillment, he has begun searching for alternatives. Luckily for him, a coworker tells him of a new approach to tackling debt, a way that just might be the solution he's been searching for. Without hesitation, Michael begins his Digital

Revolution and dives headfirst into the new world of passive income. He begins generating $500 per month in profit within six months. He realizes that when he applies his new income directly to his mortgage in addition to his minimum monthly payment, he will be able to pay off his house ten years earlier and save $88,466 in interest alone! Additionally, he calculates that he'll net an extra $58,887 in cash over the 30-year period, instead of being $542,880 in the negative. Since he's done it once, and his single stream of new income is requiring little maintenance on a weekly basis, he quickly realizes he should duplicate his efforts in order to expedite his freedom. He now understands that he must get rid of his mortgage payment as quickly as possible to live life on his own terms. Michael sees that he could potentially create as many streams of additional income as he wants, so he wastes no time creating his second and scaling up his first. Hope has been restored! The possibility of liberty is now on the table for Michael. With some hard work and automation, Michael can still take advantage of his time in Q2 and Q3 of his Clock of Life.

THE CATCH-22 OF OUR TIME

The overarching problem this book aims to solve for an individual is their lack of free time. Naturally, this lack of time is the greatest hurdle people face when they decide to start an online business. How can someone with little time to spare already expect to find the time to start an online business with no prior experience? This is surely one of the most tremendous Catch-22s of our time.

The answer is threefold. You must be willing to change your habits, you must have the proper motivation, and you mustn't expect immediate results. These are not get-rich quick schemes; instead, these are legitimate businesses designed for the long-haul. Everyone knows that great things take time, but few are willing to make the necessary sacrifices or understand delayed gratification well enough to produce the outcomes they desire. In the following paragraphs, I'll dissect each portion of the solution to the time Catch-22 mentioned above.

As I briefly mentioned in the last chapter, the people who are taking advantage of the Digital Revolution are more focused on creating rather than consuming. They realized they had to change their habits to produce the time they needed to make the transformation they desired. What does that mean? It means instead of coming home from work, feeling sorry for yourself, and turning on the TV, you open your personal computer and go to work for yourself. It means understanding this way of living is not permanent, but it's necessary to get where you want to go. It means not spending money on trivial things like alcohol and expensive meals when you could be spending those same dollars on digital advertising to figure out what you're doing. It means turning down social obligations in favor of staying home to put in the necessary work to create a different life for yourself. It means spending more time creating digital content rather than consuming it. Little shifts like this add up over time until something gives. Trust me when I tell you that you might have to seemingly disappear for a while to start a successful online business while working full-time. Consistent sacrifices will eventually turn into the results you want, but you must begin consistently practicing delayed gratification first. This is the hardest aspect to overcome, and it's extremely difficult to provide coaching on this matter. The best way I know to get over this hurdle is to start with proper motivation.

Possessing the proper motivation means beginning with a strong "why." Without a strong why, you won't stand a fighting chance of changing your habits and finding the time necessary to create a passive online business. In other words, your motivation must be greater than your laziness. When my Digital Revolution began, I didn't have a clue what I was doing, and I had no experience creating an online business. I was also working 12- to 14-hour days already. Years later, I can confidently tell you that there's no way I would've persisted through the countless roadblocks and failures had I not been standing on a rock-solid why. I knew my life numbers, I knew my family needed me, I knew I was miserable, I knew it was possible, and I desired financial freedom more than anything because I knew it would enable me to create a more meaningful life for myself. I was willing to do whatever it took to get to the point where I could wake up every day and choose my reality. The other component of possessing the proper motivation is being personally invested in your own success. For me, this was the $3,000 I invested in the professional digital advertising course that has effectively changed my life. I can recall some hard times telling myself there's no way I was letting that three grand go to waste. Without some serious skin in the game, I might not have had the motivation to push through.

The last component of the solution to the time Catch-22 is not to expect immediate results. The reason I used six months to achieve consistent $500 profit per month in the examples above is because that is a reasonable period for someone to change their habits. Additionally, knowing what it takes to learn the foundational skills and platforms necessary to begin producing passive income online, six months just makes sense. This type of transformation is not made overnight. Oddly, it'll take time to convince yourself that you deserve the success and the liberty that comes with it. In the future, when you begin doubting yourself and second guessing your efforts, return to the following paragraph on fear from one of my favorite books by Steven Pressfield—*The War of Art.*

> *Resistance feeds on fear. We experience resistance as fear. But fear of what? Fear of the consequences of following our heart. Fear of bankruptcy, fear of poverty, fear of insolvency. Fear of groveling when we try to make it on our own, and of groveling when we give up and come crawling back to where we started. Fear of being selfish, of being rotten wives or disloyal husbands; fear of failing to support our families, of sacrificing their dreams for ours. Fear of betraying our race, our 'hood, our homies. Fear of failure. Fear of being ridiculous. Fear of throwing away the education, the training, the preparation that those we love have*

sacrificed so much for, that we ourselves have worked our butts off for. Fear of launching into the void, of hurtling too far out there; fear of passing some point of no return, beyond which we cannot recant, cannot reverse, cannot rescind, but must live with this cocked-up choice for the rest of our lives. Fear of madness. Fear of insanity. Fear of death. These are serious fears. But they're not the real fear. Not the Master Fear, the Mother of all Fears that's so close to us that even when we verbalize it, we don't believe it. FEAR THAT WE WILL SUCCEED. That we can access the powers we secretly know we possess. That we can become the person we sense in our hearts we truly are.

MY FIJIAN BREAKTHROUGH

In early March of 2019, I was in Fiji—one and a half months into a seven-month circumnavigation of our beautiful planet. At this point, I had a few small streams of passive income setup, and I was focused on scaling them so I could completely cover my travel costs and continue to build my savings account. As I attempted to scale and manage each stream simultaneously, I quickly realized I needed a recorded process to follow for each venture, something to guide me each time I needed to complete a certain task or create a new stream of income. I also realized it would save me a lot of time to have everything I needed to create, manage, and scale each venture all in one place. The goal was to make it foolproof so I could do the upfront work myself, and then hand my recorded processes to a VA (virtual assistant) to manage so I could effectively focus on scaling, creating other businesses, and living my version of an extraordinary life.

My time in Fiji was important for a few reasons. First and foremost, I got the chance to live on a remote island for a week, where I got to interact with some of the most amazing people I've met on my travels. As a first-time full-time traveler, I was just beginning to realize that new introductions generally produce the exact same two questions regardless of where you are in the world. The first question you can expect is always the same: where are you from? In my experience, the second question is typically: what do you do? As I went through these introductions on that remote island in Fiji, I had a breakthrough. I would always answer the first question by saying that I'm from Texas, simple as that. In contrast, I was still learning how to answer the second question, since I'd just undergone a radical lifestyle redesign and was, frankly, doing a lot of things.

The answer that I had been giving people over the previous six weeks was the same one I gave that day: "I am a photographer who travels full-time for enjoyment while building and scaling online businesses to support myself." Unanimously, the response was always the same: "Oh my gosh, that's amazing! I'd absolutely love to do something like that, but I have no idea where to start." On the third time I heard that answer, it came like a slap in the face, and I immediately realized that I could create a one-stop shop for online business creation, management, and scaling, both for my own use and for others'. But it wasn't until later in my seven-month lap around the world that I actually decided to do it. Hilariously, I had that exact same conversation four more times, for a total of seven (yes, I kept track of them all). Today, I'm proud to tell people that I can solve their problem of not knowing where to start. And not only that, I can give them everything else they need to create passive income online for themselves in not just one way, but five.

My solution comes in the form of a seven-week online passive income program called Three Sevens named for the seven-week nature of the program, my seven-month lap around the world, and the seven identical conversations that compelled me to create the program in the first place. Within the program, I've answered the *Who, What, Where, When, Why,* and *How* for each of the five ventures included. In the following chapter, I'll dive into the details of each of my five modes of passive income. You'll learn what each venture consists of through an executive summary, exactly how much each venture costs to start, and the step-by-step creation process for each from idea to profit.

CHAPTER 8

Five Ways to Create Passive Income Online

I KNOW OF NOTHING MORE DESPICABLE AND
PATHETIC THAN A MAN WHO DEVOTES ALL
THE HOURS OF THE WAKING DAY TO THE
MAKING OF MONEY FOR MONEY'S SAKE.

John D. Rockefeller

Before we get into the five ways to create passive income that are contained in my Three Sevens Program, pause for a moment and give me your best guess for how many satellites you think are orbiting the earth. This is a question I love to ask because it forces a person to recognize how advanced our civilization is. By better understanding our collective capabilities, a person gains self-confidence in the technological arena. In my experience, most people think the number is somewhere between 100 and 1,000, but they have no clue. Honestly, I had no earthly idea either until I performed a simple Google search. In early 2019, the United Nations Office for Outer Space Affairs (UNOOSA) reported in their Index of Objects Launched into Outer Space that there were 4,987 satellites orbiting the earth. Can you imagine how much collective human effort went into getting each of those satellites off the ground, out of our atmosphere and successfully into orbit? I don't know about you, but if it were left up to me, I wouldn't know where to start with even one satellite, let alone almost 5,000. Fortunately for me, it doesn't matter; I get to take advantage of them either way. This is the same lens we need to look at the internet through. We are so fortunate to be alive in 2020 and able to capitalize on the collective human efforts that came before us.

There are multitudes of astounding tools and platforms available online that took so much collective human effort to produce, yet, individually, we don't need to know the first thing about creating them since they already exist. Thankfully for us, the tools we need to create passive income are user-friendly and either very inexpensive or completely free. Because of this, the barrier for entry has been lowered dramatically. It is now easier than ever to start an online business, and you will see shortly that anyone with a solid Wi-Fi connection and the motivation to do so can have a legit business up and running in a matter of weeks. This is surely a new concept for many people, and I'm sure some of you are hearing the voice in your head spewing doubts, since you've been conditioned to be dependent on an organization your entire life. Don't worry, doubts (as well as your debt) are about to get squashed by innovation.

Keep in mind each of the five ways I'm about to present are all legitimate online businesses designed by me to be passive in nature. These processes are the result of many iterations, and I've spent years and tens of thousands of dollars testing and refining each approach until I was able to produce consistent results. Don't ask me how many other venture models I tried before settling on these! Essentially, I've taken an engineering approach to creating each venture model, beginning with the end in mind. The design criteria for each venture was creating the ability to remove myself from the day-to-day equation but retaining ownership of the business and the associated profits.

Before we get into the venture details, please recognize that there will likely be terms you don't understand within each venture type below. Rest assured, Week 1 of the program is dedicated to teaching you all the skills and knowledge necessary to utilize all the tools and terms contained in Week 2 through Week 7. Additionally, since my online businesses are built on the foundation of digital marketing, naturally the first week of the program (Week 1) is dedicated to teaching the same skills that I invested thousands of dollars to attain years ago. You'll learn everything I know about paid advertising and turning money into more money through Facebook Ads and Google Ads. Paid digital advertising is the most important skill you'll learn in Week 1, but you'll also learn niche selection, demand verification, brand building, website creation, funnel setup, traffic procurement, and email marketing. Week 1 will enable you to market yourself as a digital advertising specialist with a whole new set of skills that are crucial to any business. Effectively, you'll be able to perform your own business's marketing efforts or get paid to perform digital advertising services for other businesses. When I grasped the potential this skill set affords, I had no choice but to go for it myself. I'm glad I did!

Furthermore, understand that some of these things might be new and unknown to you, but I assure you, most people with basic computer skills and a low-level understanding of Microsoft Excel can create a new source of income following these processes. The reality is most people who want to start an online business today don't have to worry about overcoming a massive technological hurdle. If you use social media, you can use the tools required to create automated online businesses. Additionally, if you find yourself confused or at a roadblock, each necessary tool is thoroughly explained in the Tools & Resources section of each of the five core weeks. Lastly, how to perform each step in each venture process is thoroughly explained within the program.

It is no longer necessary to settle for a lousy existence in order to make a living. There are thousands of ways to make money online, and I applaud all those who are teaching others to do so too. However, these are the five venture models that I've had success with and teach in the Three Sevens Passive Income Program. Think of each of the five ventures as a standalone business. Let's dive in!

VENTURE 1—LOCAL BUSINESS ADVERTISING (WEEK 2)

Executive Summary

There are 30.2 million local businesses in America, and less than 1% of them advertise on Facebook. They don't have the time, and they don't know how, but they want more customers, and you could be the one that steps in and handles their digital marketing effort.

The basic idea here is to automate a lead-generation process via Facebook ad for a specific discounted offer at a local business and then strike a deal with the business to charge them $15 per lead you produce for them. A "lead" in this case is synonymous with "new customer." You are generating new customers for a local business and the local business is paying you $15 per new customer you send them.

To generate leads, you'll be advertising a discount coupon on Facebook for a specific offer at a local business. When someone clicks your Facebook ad, they'll be taken to a simple landing page where they exchange their contact information for the coupon. When they submit their info, they'll be automatically emailed the coupon and directions for how to use it. Each week, you'll email your accumulated leads to your client and get paid $15 per lead at the end of the month. I've illustrated the simple funnel you'll be creating to generate leads below:

Facebook ad → Simple landing page for coupon claiming (lead captured) → Auto email issuing coupon and directions for redemption to lead → Local business pays you per lead

Why does this work?

1—**Potential lifetime value.** Each coupon claimed is a chance for the local business to earn someone's business in repeat fashion. In other words, many local businesses are willing to lose money on the first customer interaction to gain their business in the long run.

2—**Cost savings for the local businesses using Groupon for lead generation.** Since you are only selecting already proven offers from Groupon (see Venture Process below) and you know that Groupon takes 50% of the sale right off the top, you automatically know the cost of new customer acquisition your potential client is getting using Groupon. This gives you the inside scoop and allows you to market your service appropriately. You are providing the same service as Groupon (producing new customers for local businesses) but you are doing it for far less money.

Total startup cost: $70

• Initial Facebook ad spend - $49
• Website + professional email - $21

Venture Process

Step 1 – Select a target city
Step 2 – Use Groupon to select a proven offer
Step 3 – Verify the local business is NOT running Facebook ads
Step 4 – Create a simple coupon for the selected offer
Step 5 – Create a simple two-step funnel for the selected offer
Step 6 – Set up email autoresponder for coupon issuing
Step 7 – Create a Facebook ad for the selected proven offer and run traffic for seven days ($7/day budget) to acquire leads
Step 8 – Pause the ad and approach the business with free leads
Step 9 – Strike a deal with the local business for your lead-generation service

As soon as you have a service agreement in place, the local business will pay for the Facebook ad budget. At that point, all you need to do is return to the initial Facebook ad you setup, adjust the budget per your agreement, and press resume. You will then get paid $15 every time someone claims your coupon and you are no longer spending your own money on ads.

What a single stream of profit looks like:

Profit = Agency Fees ($15/lead) - Startup Costs - Ongoing Costs

Ongoing (monthly) costs include:

- Website – $15
- Professional email hosting service – $6

If you follow my system, just one client with an ad budget of between $500 and $1,000 per month should produce between 45 and 90 leads. This equates to $675–1,350 in profit per month on autopilot for you at $15 per lead.

Venture Scaling Options

- You can run as many initial client-targeting Facebook campaigns as you'd like. This only increases your chances of success because, like anything else, this is a numbers game—the more businesses you approach with free leads, the more clients you'll win. Don't be afraid to invest your earnings back into the business. That is the best way to scale this venture. For every $100 you make, that's two potential clients you could seduce, or more. As soon as you get that first one, you should be putting all that income into getting as many more clients as you can.

- Once the amount of leads you are producing per month costs the local business more than their initial established budget, it'll make sense for the business owner to agree to a lump sum monthly agency fee instead of a fee per lead. Once you get to this point, you're offering your client savings in exchange for automated billing. The current market rate for this service is between $1,000 and $3,000 per month.
- Create a case study based on the results you produced for your first client. Send this to every other local business in your niche in America with an introductory video and your auto scheduler link to sign up for a phone call with you to discuss how you can produce the same results for them.
- Create another advertising agency in another niche (rinse and repeat).

VENTURE 2—AFFILIATE MARKETING (WEEK 3)

Executive Summary

According to 99firms, annual affiliate marketing commissions are projected to hit the $6.8 billion mark in 2020.

In this venture model, you serve as the bridge between a buyer and a seller. You do not have any products of your own; you are marketing for other businesses and services in exchange for a commission on sales that you bring to them.

Ever wonder how bloggers make money? This is it. Bloggers build an audience by providing value around a specific topic within a niche. Every link you see within a blog or article is generally affiliate marketed. If you were to click on a link within a blog that takes you to an external site and you make a purchase, a percentage of the purchase price would go to the blog owner for referring you to the seller.

This can be an extremely lucrative venture model because you don't have many headaches compared to some other business models. Having no products means no customer service, no returns, no inventory management, and no product cost—among other things. Also, once a link is setup, there is generally no future management involved—just potential profit. It also takes relatively no money to begin.

Affiliate marketing is one of the best ways to monetize an audience, but most people don't know you don't need to have an existing audience to start affiliate marketing. The goal is to build an audience to provide value to and there are proven ways to quickly start from scratch.

Content is king in this venture model. The goal is to produce engaging content that is valuable to a reader as it relates to his/her interests. You want to establish yourself as an authority and expert within your niche so that when you recommend a product or service to your audience, they know it's legit and they'll want to check it out.

Note: It's important to choose a niche that is legitimately interesting to you so you don't have to pull your hair out to research it and create content within it as you grow your brand. I've tried to enter niches that I thought would be profitable before, but I quickly realized I just couldn't do the work because I wasn't interested in what I was writing about.

I should also mention there are solid ways to outsource the content creation, but they're not free. (These are covered in depth within the program.)

The most efficient way to affiliate market is a combination of creating a blog and utilizing email marketing. Once your blog is setup and you have at least three posts created, you'll need a couple relevant lead magnets to begin generating traffic. The goal is to convert that website traffic into purchases via the links you will embed into your blog as recommendations and personal experiences.

You will then repurpose the content from your blog to setup your email marketing campaigns. The goal within the email campaigns is the exact same as with the traffic on your blog—to convert readers into buyers for the products/services you are affiliate marketing.

This is a numbers game just like many of the other venture options within the program. The more people that visit your site, the higher the likelihood is that one will convert into a buyer through one of your affiliate links. In the same breath, the larger your email list, the higher the likelihood is that your email marketing will produce affiliate sales.

To summarize, your two money making platforms are your website (blog) and your email marketing campaigns to your subscribers (who you will gain through your lead magnets at first).

Total startup cost: $46

- Domain – $15
- Professional Logo – $15 (or free via Squarespace free logo maker if you choose)
- Website – $16

Venture Process

Step 1 – Select a niche to build an audience in

Step 2 – Identify products and services within your niche to affiliate market

Step 3 – Set up affiliate marketing deals and procure affiliate links

Step 4 – Create your website and three blog posts for your selected niche

Step 5 – Create two relevant and desirable lead magnets for your niche

Step 6 – Set up auto email marketing campaigns

Step 7 – Create organic traffic using your lead magnets, SEO strategies, collaborations, and social media

Step 8 (optional) – Run retargeting ads on Facebook and Instagram promoting new content to organic site visitors

Step 9 (optional) – Run Facebook and Instagram ads using your lead magnets to capture emails and drive traffic to your blog

Step 10 (optional) – Run Google ads for your blog posts to drive traffic to your blog

What a single stream of profit looks like:

Profit = Affiliate Commissions - Startup Costs - Ongoing Costs

Ongoing (monthly) costs include:

- Website – $15

Results vary widely based on your selected niche and the products and services you decide to market, although according to 99firms, 52% of affiliate marketers make more than $20,000 per year which equates to about $1,667 per month.

Venture Scaling Options

- Scaling your blogging effort can be summarized as the optional Steps 8 through 10. In short, when you get to the point where you're generating affiliate commissions organically, it makes so much sense to reinvest those earnings into Steps 8 through 10 in the "Venture Process."
- Secure collaborations with other authority figures in your niche to increase your exposure to your target audience.
- Create another blog in another niche (rinse and repeat).

VENTURE 3—HIGH-TICKET DROP-SHIPPING (WEEK 4)

Executive Summary

According to 99firms, by 2040, around 95% of all purchases are expected to be via eCommerce. This means that now is the time to get in and claim a niche for yourself.

Drop-shipping is a retail fulfillment method that allows you to sell items without owning or storing any inventory. There are many ways to use the drop-shipping model, but for the purposes of my program we focus on what we call high-ticket drop-shipping. High-ticket drop-shipping is simply setting up a business to sell only items worth $500 or more.

In this model, a customer will buy a product from your website, then you will immediately buy the item directly from the manufacturer for less, and the manufacturer will ship the item directly to the buyer. You serve as the middleman who connects a buyer and a seller, and you keep the difference between what you advertise the item for and what you buy it from the supplier for (retail vs. wholesale). Your goal is to sell high and buy low. To do this, you must learn how to enter into wholesale agreements with premium U.S.-based suppliers. You'll learn exactly how to do this efficiently and consistently within the program.

Drop-shipping requires no upfront cost to sell expensive products, since you are being paid before you make any inventory purchases yourself.

Total startup cost: $236

- Shopify Store – $29
- Domain – Starting at $11 from Shopify
- Professional logo – $15
- Professional email (G-Suite) – $6
- Corporation formation – $150

- Google ads – $100 credit with signup for Google AdWords
- Facebook retargeting ads – $25

Venture Process

Step 1 – Select a high-ticket niche category
Step 2 – Create a Shopify store for your selected niche category
Step 3 – Secure supplier approval and create reseller accounts
Step 4 – Set up auto email campaigns to prepare to market to your email list
Step 5 – Launch your store and run traffic (both organically and paid)
Step 6 – Set up retargeting ads on Facebook and Instagram

What a single stream of profit looks like:

Profit = Revenue - COGS - AD Spend - Start-up Costs - Ongoing Costs

COGS = Cost of Goods Sold

- Includes shipping and any other supplier fees

Ongoing (monthly) costs include:

- Shopify fee – $29
- Email hosting service – $6

Using my process, a single high-ticket drop-shipping store is designed to make one sale per day that nets at least $50 in profit.

Venture Scaling Options

- Secure additional supplier approvals to add more premium/quality products to your store.
- Use profits to increase ad budgets. More qualified site visitors = more conversions = more sales!
- Create another store in another niche (rinse and repeat).

VENTURE 4—DIGITAL PRODUCT SALES (WEEK 5)

Executive Summary

Selling digital products is one of the best ways to generate truly passive income. You create something once, and it can be sold millions of times without any more work on your end.

With the nature of a digital product, there are many perks including:

- They last forever.
- Product is never out of stock.
- No shipping and handling costs or logistics.
- No product storage fees.
- Extremely low return rate and customer service required.
- Relatively no ongoing business management.
- Irresistible profit margins and unlimited potential income.
- The internet is a huge market and easily accessible.
- Extremely low overhead costs.
- Once you create your product, anyone can buy it, anywhere in the world, at anytime.

Selling digital products is one of the best ways to create what is commonly known as a lifestyle business. There are many different forms of digital products, but they all MUST be geared towards helping someone achieve a specific result that they desire.

Digital products are completely value driven. The goal is to create something that a group of people will be able to use to solve a problem, make a change, or achieve a specific result. Digital products are essentially just information packaged in a variety of different ways. The more valuable the information and possible personal transformation, the higher the price the product is justified to be.

There are high-ticket digital products and low-ticket digital products. High-ticket products are any products that are priced over $2,000. As a rule of thumb, anything under $2,000 doesn't require a phone call to close the deal. Anything over $2,000 usually requires a phone call to close the deal, although this can be overcome with things such as webinars and high-quality videos explaining the product in detail.

Apart from the price and possible phone call required, there is little difference in the process for creating a successful high-ticket offer versus a low-ticket offer.

Total startup cost: $46

- Professional Logo – $15
- Domain – $15
- Website – $16

Venture Process

Step 1 – Identify a problem that many people are experiencing
Step 2 – Decide what kind of digital product will create the best solution
Step 3 – Create the digital product and set up the fulfillment method
Step 4 – Create a sales page (website) for your digital product
Step 5 – Create two lead magnets associated with the problem/ solution
Step 6 – Set up auto-email marketing campaigns
Step 7 – Run paid ads using your lead magnets and digital product
Step 8 – Set up retargeting ads and organic growth methods

What a single stream of profit looks like:

Profit = Revenue - Ad Spend - Ongoing Costs

Ongoing (monthly) costs include:

- Website –$16
- Email hosting service –$6
- Product delivery platform (optional)

There are many types of digital products that range from low-ticket ebooks and PDFs to high-ticket transformational programs and courses. Depending on which type of digital product you choose and the associated transformation you are selling, profit per month can range from a few hundred dollars to tens of thousands of dollars.

Venture Scaling Options

- Create additional desirable lead magnets to attract new people into your funnel.
- Use your initial profits to increase ad budgets to reach more people.
- Create a blog in your digital product's niche to drive additional traffic to your website organically via SEO (search engine optimization) efforts.
- Secure collaborations with other authority figures in your niche to increase your exposure to your target audience.
- Create another digital product in the same niche or another niche (rinse and repeat).

VENTURE 5—AMAZON PRIVATE LABEL FBA (FULFILLED BY AMAZON) (WEEK 6)

Executive Summary

According to CNBC, Amazon sold more than 175 million items during Prime Day in 2019!

Private labeling is essentially taking existing products and rebranding them to sell under your own brand. This approach allows you to sell a tested and vetted product under your own label. A great example you probably know of already is Walmart's private label brand—Great Value. You'll find a Great Value version of almost everything in the store. Walmart is not manufacturing all those products themselves; they've simply contracted with many different suppliers to create products with their label on it. They've effectively leveraged many manufactures to have quality and inexpensive offerings across many markets—all within the same store with the same recognized label.

When you create a private label business on Amazon, you select a product that is already a proven seller. Then you brand, differentiate/improve the product and sell it as your own. This gives you control over the quality, supply, price, the listing on Amazon, and everything else associated with the product's details.

Not only is Amazon one of the top retailers in the world, they have superior customer service, a proven track record, and an unparalleled user experience. They are one of the most trusted names in households across the world and competing for the top search engine spot next to Google. This means when someone needs something, their first instinct may be to open Amazon and search for it rather than searching on Google.

With the Amazon platform already having millions of daily users, you don't have to worry about driving traffic to your own website. Plus, Amazon FBA offers the simplicity of having fulfillment warehouses to store your goods, and the service of having your orders fulfilled. You get all the benefits of being a business owner without storing inventory, managing workers, or making trips to the post office.

As soon as you have all your products delivered to an Amazon warehouse, the venture is essentially passive, since Amazon handles customer service, product advertising, and shipping your items when sold.

Once you have this process down, you can expect to put about 40 hours in on the front end to produce a private label product and have it available for sale on Amazon. This is a miniscule investment when you understand the income potential and passive structure of the venture. You should get to the point where you are putting in 40 hours over the course of two to three months, then making passive income for years. All you'll have to do is press the re-order button with your manufacturer and freight forwarder once you've done it the first time.

Note: there are also some possible weekly tasks in Amazon Seller Central, such as return management, answering customer questions, and adjusting your advertising strategy, but all of this can be outsourced very easily once you have the initial product setup.

Total startup cost: $1,500+

- Product samples – $100 minimum (just pay shipping generally)
- Product fabrication – Varies largely, but most MOQ's (minimum order quantities) are at least 250 items and the minimum cost for a worthwhile product will likely be at least $2 each, so you're looking at about $500 minimum for this line item.
- Product shipping (from manufacturer to Amazon warehouse) – There are three basic shipping options that vary largely in price, but the cheapest option is sea freight and it costs around $1.15/lb.
- Product labels – $250 GS1 signup

- Company registration – $25
- Professional product logo graphic design – $15
- Product photography – $150 to $400

Venture Process

Step 1 – Identify a profitable niche and select a proven product

Step 2 – Contact suppliers and order product samples

Step 3 – Estimate total start-up costs for your selected product

Step 4 – Create your brand & request final product samples

Step 5 – Select a manufacturer and send down payment to begin fabrication

Step 6 – Arrange shipping services with a freight forwarder

Step 7 – Finalize the product listing on Amazon

Step 8 – Launch your product

What a single stream of profit looks like:

Profit = Revenue - (COGS + Startup Costs + Amazon Fees + Ongoing Costs)

COGS = cost of goods sold

Amazon fees include:

- Fulfillment fee (depends on the product size and category)
- Referral fee (most likely 15% of purchase price per sale)
- Product storage/warehouse fees (depends on the product volume)

Ongoing (monthly) costs include:

- Amazon Professional Seller Account fee – $39

My system is designed to find product opportunities with both high demand and low competition. By following the guidelines as set forth in the program, a successful product opportunity will make at least $10 per sale. The goal is to get to the point where you are making at least five sales per day as quickly as possible ($50 per day). With some clever product launch techniques and automated review soliciting follow-ups, this is achievable.

Venture Scaling Options

- Strategic reordering of inventory. This means knowing your monthly sales volume and how long it will take you to replenish inventory. Typically, with 30 days of fabrication and 30 days of sea shipping, you'll be 60 to 70 days out once you reorder inventory. You must reorder the inventory in advance so you don't run out of stock and miss out on sales. Running out of inventory can also impact your best-seller ranking, so this is important to monitor. This involves projecting sales two months down the road since your lead time for new products is 60 to 70 days.
- Creating variations of this product such as color, bundles, size, etc. On top of your initial product, you can work with the manufacture to add to this product's offering by creating variations. Creating the same product in a different color is the easiest way to create a variation, but creating a bundle (set of two, set of set, etc.) and creating a different size can also be very effective ways to diversify your product offering.
- Creating additional products to compliment this product under the same private label (think "frequently bought together"). What products could you offer that would complement your first product that would cause someone to purchase them together? This can be a great way to build your new brand in your niche.
- Utilizing Amazon's paid advertising campaigns.

For your knowledge, Week 2 through Week 6 in the program are structured as followed:

1. Startup cost breakdown
2. Executive summary
   - Explains the basics of what the venture is and how to do it
3. Venture plan (WHAT to do, WHEN and WHY)
   - Explains the step-by-step process in depth from idea to profit
4. Tools and Resources (HOW to do WHAT)
   - Teaches you which tools you need and exactly how to use them as they pertain to the specific venture
5. Three Sevens featured example (HOW to put it all together)
   - A specific step-by-step real-world example following the Venture Plan that combines everything you've learned from previous sections
6. Scaling
   - How-to scale this venture and what to expect along the way
7. Ongoing cost breakdown

It's everything you need all in one place to start your own Digital Revolution. I've removed the need to spend years and thousands of dollars figuring it all out for yourself. If you're ready to get started making money online, look no further.

I'd be willing to bet that if your personal Digital Revolution is not already underway, it is now. Good luck sleeping tonight with all these new possibilities! Now that you grasp the importance of the ongoing Digital Revolution, you've seen the impacts of passive income on debt, and you have no excuse for not knowing where to start, let's transition to my second solution for achieving ultimate freedom—tiny living. In the following chapter, we'll look at what tiny living is, analyze the tremendous tiny movement that's sweeping the globe, and I'll explain why on earth someone would want to live in a tiny home.

PART III

Tiny Living

CHAPTER 9

Tiny Home = Tiny Mortgage = Financial Freedom

BETTER TO LIVE IN A RUGGED LAND AND
RULE THAN TO CULTIVATE RICH LANDS
AND BE A SLAVE.

Cyrus the Great

I t's not the unnecessary space that makes each of our modern homes equivalent to an ancient kingdom, but the comforts and technological capabilities each one possesses within. In almost every modern American home, you'll find a machine keeping food fresh for months on end, endless clean running water, hot water on demand, a gadget that spits out cubes of ice, a device that heats food with the press of a button, a fully controlled comfortable climate, and unlimited power (gas or electricity). Not even one of these modern conveniences that we take for granted were available to the kings and queens of ancient empires, although they had a different kind of unlimited power. Most of these comforts weren't even available two hundred years ago. In fact, one of the most notable modern kingdoms that exists, the White House, didn't receive running water until 1833.

Just as our way of life has changed dramatically over the millennia without each generation realizing it, our individual level of comfort has also been increasing exponentially without us taking a minute to stop and think about it. Effectively, we are each modern-day kings and queens in our own right …

This is the lens to look at tiny living through.

What do I mean by "tiny living"? Tiny living can be thought of as an intentional, minimalistic mode of consumption combined with the modern comforts we all know and love. By living tiny, we can enjoy the comforts of a modern kingdom while enabling ourselves to live a life aligned with our passions and purpose.

There are many ways to live tiny. Really, it's more of an ideology rather than a set way of living. For me, my transition from an uptown Dallas apartment to tiny living began in late 2018 with getting out of my lease, selling all my furniture, and getting rid of most my clothes and possessions. At that point, I could officially carry all my belongings at once. Undeniably, I am on the extreme end of the tiny living spectrum. I don't have a home, so I am at home wherever I am, yet I am always comfortable with a roof over my head, and I enjoy the same modern comforts that most people do. This works well for me at this stage in my life for my current desired lifestyle and desired impact. Living tiny enables me to travel the world doing what I love, rather than forcing myself into a demanding job to make a lot of money just to afford an average apartment or mortgage. It enables me to have ultimate flexibility that drastically reduces my cost of living, since I can take advantage of the cheapest flight deals available and reserve apartments and rooms months in advance at huge discounts. Therefore, having less enables me to need less money to live and to do more of the things that bring me joy and fulfillment—it's a win-win. I should note that I'm not some high roller staying in penthouse apartments, flying first class, and driving around in fancy cars. I've intentionally made some sacrifices to gain full-time freedom.

A TINY MAGICAL MOVEMENT

Within the tiny living ideology, there is a comparatively small but magical movement currently sweeping the globe. It's comprised of people who give more than they take, people who live intentionally with passion and purpose, and people who grasp the concept of having more with less. These are people that have had enough of the materialistic cycle, people that put their foot down and said, "today I reclaim my life." They are inspiring to say the least. The movement is the Tiny Home Movement, and you could consider it a tiny revolution. Most people react in one of two ways when they first learn about this fantastic new living option:

1. No way I'd want to live in something so small; I like my space.
2. Those are the coolest little houses I've ever seen! How much do they cost and how do I get one?

More often than not, if you're in group one, once you see an episode or two of *Living Big* In A *Tiny House* on YouTube, *Tiny House Nation* on Netflix, or *Tiny House, Big Living* on HGTV, you'll either change your mind, or end up understanding how people actually do it. But are you really grasping the concept here? These people aren't out there to get attention. They're out there living their versions of the American Dream, and other people can't get enough of it. These people have sweet liberty, and they're living a life consistent with the intent our Founding Fathers established. Living in a tiny home oftentimes grants a person financial freedom automatically! THAT IS THE CONCEPT.

LIBERATION IS A CHOICE

Before we get into the multitude of benefits produced by tiny living, we must first explore the financial benefits of tiny-home living. Just like anything else, tiny-home living is a conscious choice. Anyone can choose to live in a tiny home rather than in a traditional American-size home. To demonstrate the incredible life-altering power of the financial benefits, let's return to our friend Michael's life situation.

Recall that Michael has already purchased a typical American home with a starting mortgage value of $309,200. In Chapter 3, you learned that as soon as Michael made the choice to purchase his home, he became a slave to his mortgage payment, since he had to produce at least $1,508 per month for 30 years. Let's look at how the financial trajectory of Michael's life can change if he chooses tiny-home living instead of tradition. To begin, understand that you can buy a professionally built, fully furnished, move-in ready tiny home for as little as $15,000. That is as small and inexpensive as they get, unless you elect to build it yourself. That number also doesn't include any land or site preparation, but we'll get into those two other components in Chapter 11. For this example, we're going to assume Michael can hire a professional tiny-home builder to build his home, procure his own land, and get the site ready, all for $65,000. This is more than doable, and I'll walk you through the steps to make this happen for yourself in the following chapters.

Many of the professional tiny-home builders offer in-house financing with interest rates slightly less favorable than traditional mortgages but with payback periods that are significantly shorter. Since Michael has decent credit, he's able to lock in a 15-year payback period, a 5.5% interest rate and 15% down payment with a premium builder. This equates to a minimum monthly payment of $459, which is a savings of over $1,000 per month compared to his previous living situation. On top of that, if he paid only the minimum monthly payment, he'd be looking at only 15 years of mortgage debt rather than the 30 years he initially signed up for. He will still pay an additional $27,370 in interest alone over the 15-year period, but this is a far cry from the $233,680 he would've paid in interest over 30 years with his traditional mortgage. In scenario one, his total cost to put a roof over his head was $542,880 over 30 years. In scenario two, the total cost to put a roof over his head is $82,620 over just 15 years.

As if that isn't enough, there is another trick Michael can implement to combat the amount of interest he'll pay. Since he was three years into his traditional mortgage and faithfully paying at least the minimum monthly amount, and it thankfully didn't depreciate in the three years that he "owned" it, he has some equity in his house. He still owed close to $300,000, but he was able to sell it for a similar amount to the original purchase price, pocketing almost $44,000. If he applies just $35,000 of this profit to his new down payment, even if he only paid the $459 monthly payment going forward, he will have his tiny home paid off in just 5 years. Furthermore, he'd only pay $3,015 in interest rather than the $27,370 he would've paid over his 15-year deal. Michael has found one of the quickest ways to gain financial freedom by ditching the current version of the American Dream and living in an unnecessarily large house.

Michael has chosen to liberate himself with a simple lifestyle change. Since he no longer needs $1,508 per month just to cover his mortgage, he effectively no longer needs such a demanding job. Since he has less, he needs less monthly to support himself. He now has the freedom to choose to keep working his job or do something more aligned with his purpose and personal aspirations. He now can trade work projects for personal projects; morning/evening commutes for personal healthcare; pointless meetings for friends and family; deadlines for freedom; and rushing for intentional living. Comparatively, the people that are living large in tiny homes are cut from the same cloth as the people who would still go to work tomorrow if they knew they were no longer getting paid. Both groups of people share one important characteristic: they work for meaning and impact, not money. This means that their lives are structured in a way that allows them to do so. They have their basic financial needs met so they can focus on work that matters to them instead of living paycheck to paycheck to afford things that are truly unnecessary.

THE FLOOD IS COMING

Not surprisingly, some of the smartest Americans (on paper) have figured this out first. In fact, according to tinyhousetalk.com, people currently living in a tiny home in the U.S. are twice as likely to have a master's degree than their traditional home living counterparts. So, what happens when the rest of the U.S. population figures this out? Yes, the same people that are stressed out of their minds, unfulfilled, unhealthy, exhausted, and burnt out. I believe we are at the very beginning of a Housing Revolution as the word about the life benefits of tiny home living start to get out. Tiny homes will innovate the housing market in the same way that the internet is innovating education, commerce, and retirement. When people realize that this is a quick way to eliminate the need to work a dead-end job for 40 years, they will be more than willing to sacrifice their space. Space is simply not worth the sacrifice of your life for a cause you most likely don't care about anyways. Additionally, when people realize that tiny home living enables liberty, fulfillment, and a life full of doing whatever they desire, there will be a flood of people knocking on the tiny door of the revolution. For this reason, I guarantee that the tiny home movement is neither a trend nor a fad—it's here to stay. At some point in the future, it just might become the norm. Mark my words, when the flood begins, the people who sell their traditional homes first will be the winners and the people who deliberate will be trapped without a buyer. The winners will be free, and the losers will be stuck at their jobs so they can pay for their space. The Clock of Life is ticking.

When it comes down to it, there are only two differences between a typical American home and a typical tiny home:

1. Size
2. Portability

In terms of modern comforts and technological capabilities, they are mostly identical. Since most tiny homes have been built within the last ten years, I would argue that they are more technologically advanced than the typical American home, but that is beside the point. The point is the main sacrifice from traditional to tiny is the amount of indoor space you lose. It's hard to see it without experiencing it for yourself, but tiny living forces a person to live with extreme intention. This is a great benefit to a person's mental health and fulfillment. Living in a small space requires a very purposeful design—a design that must factor in the things that are of utmost importance to a person. Obviously, this forces someone to choose what's important to them, and organize their life so that those things are both front of mind and front of house. It also forces someone to have much less, which helps them appreciate the things they do have and make sure those things are their absolute favorite things. I have four shirts that travel with me; you better believe they are my all-time favorite shirts. They all fit me well and are extremely comfortable. When you live with extreme intention, everything you touch is high-quality by design. This inevitably leads to a more satisfied and fulfilled existence.

TINY HOMES CREATE PASSIVE INCOME

Moreover, it doesn't take a master's degree to understand the financial possibilities associated with tiny home living. Investors big and small have started to take note and new investors are entering the tiny home market daily. The math is thrilling to say the least. Even just one tiny home, strategically placed, can produce thousands of dollars per month in passive income through popular rental platforms such as Airbnb and VRBO. For reference, a top-of-the-line tiny home costs in the range of $125,000 with a premium builder. After performing extensive research on what is available currently, I can tell you that if you want to rent a tiny home for a night, you can expect to pay between $75 and $550. The $75 nightly rate is associated with tiny homes that cost $30,000 or less, while the $550 nighty rate is associated with the premium tiny homes that cost around $125,000. Below, we'll look at four different scenarios associated with a comfortable and modern tiny home for the same $112,500 initial investment.

The initial investment consists of the following components:

- Land cost: $30,000 with 15% down and a 5% interest rate over five years
- Sitework cost: $7,500 paid upon completion
- Tiny home: $75,000 with 15% down and a 5% interest rate over 15 years

For each of the scenarios below, we are going to assume a reasonable occupancy rate of 50%, meaning that the property will be booked 50% of the time it is available. Additionally, we are going to use an average nightly rate of $200, which is a conservative estimate for our $75,000 tiny home compared with current market offerings.

Scenarios

1. 100% investment property (available for rent all 12 months per year)
   - Nightly rate: $200
   - Occupancy rate: 50%
   - Days rented per year: 180
   - Average monthly net cashflow: $2,019
   - Yearly net cashflow: $24,225
2. 67% investment property, 33% living (available for rent eight months per year, you live in it four months per year)
   - Nightly rate: $200
   - Occupancy rate: 50%
   - Days rented per year: 120
   - Average monthly net cashflow: $1,019
   - Yearly net cashflow: $12,225
3. 50% investment property, 50% living (available for rent six months per year, you live in it six months per year)

- Nightly rate: $200
- Occupancy rate: 50%
- Days rented per year: 90
- Average monthly net cashflow: $519
- Yearly net cashflow: $6,225
4. 33% investment property, 67% living (available for rent four months per year, you live in it for eight months per year)
   - Nightly rate: $200
   - Occupancy rate: 50%
   - Days rented per year: 60
   - Average monthly net cashflow: $19
   - Yearly cashflow: $225

As you can see, it's not rocket science to eliminate your housing costs. Even if you were to break even on a yearly basis, you'd still be living rent-free. Utilizing platforms like Airbnb, this is attainable regardless of which scenario above works best for you. Personally, I'd be fond of scenario two, with 67% investment purposes and 33% living, meaning I could travel for eight months per year and live in my tiny home for four months. I can't think of a better scenario than having a home for four months out of the year that pays me instead of me having to pay for it. What a concept! And don't even get me started on what a portfolio of tiny home investments looks like. Again, this is another source of potential passive income and you already know the impacts associated with that.

I'd also like to point out that there is another land component option that achieves the same financial results as shown above. Instead of purchasing a property for $30,000, you could rent space on someone else's property for $500/month or less to achieve the same net cashflows. Essentially, you'd be paying monthly rent to park somewhere and retaining your mobility instead of going into debt and putting down more permanent roots. This also drastically widens your location options, since it's much easier to place a tiny home in or near a city in this case rather than in a rural setting where land is less expensive. This is an extremely common way to satisfy the land component.

The financial impacts of going tiny are surely exciting, but by far the most important thing to consider about tiny living is what it enables you to DO with your life. This is the essence of having more with less. It's about having more of the things that spark a light in you and eliminating the things that drain you of your energy. It's about doing the things that you've always wanted to do. It's about having the time to follow your gut and trust your own intuition. It's about designing a life that enables you to work towards your personal potential and become the best you can be. In the following chapter, we'll look at what life can be like after making the decision to go tiny.

CHAPTER 10

Having More with Less

WORKING HARD FOR SOMETHING WE
DON'T CARE ABOUT IS CALLED STRESS.
WORKING HARD FOR SOMETHING WE LOVE
IS CALLED PASSION.

Simon Sinek

In the summer of 2019, I finally got to do something incredible that I had been waiting almost three years to do. To add to the magic, I got to do it with my best friend, who shared the same dream. Together, we spent two weeks exploring Singapore and one week exploring the Italian Riviera before we headed to Spain. There, we began eight weeks of living on a sailing yacht while preparing to get our Yachtmaster certifications. Our days were spent sailing up and down the coast of Spain based out of a lovely city two hours north of Barcelona called Palamós. After eight weeks of enjoyable preparation, it was a dream come true for us both to pass our final practical exam and officially claim the coveted title of Yachtmaster.

While this experience was exceptional in itself, I want to point out two things about it. Number one, my new set of skills will enrich my life for many years to come. The certification opens up many doors for work opportunities (that I hardly consider work), and I now have the confidence to either rent a sailing yacht for unbelievable vacations or own a yacht for an entirely different way of living and exploring our beautiful planet. Number two, there is no way I would've been able to achieve this while still working a full-time job. Can you imagine what most American bosses would say if you walked into their office and requested eight weeks off so you could achieve this dream? I would expect laughter and something along the lines of, "Don't let the door hit you on the way out." Since I have less, I am able to achieve more and to be more. This concept has expanded the possibilities of my life dramatically.

THE TRIFECTA (1.0)

Building on this concept, I'd like to introduce you to something that my best friend and I created, known as "The Trifecta." The Trifecta is both our current version of the American Dream and part of our definition of having more with less. This concept was born in Italy, harvested in Spain, and it will become reality in America and beyond. The idea is to have complete global mobility while retaining the ability to always be at home. We can achieve this with a combination of a tiny home, a premium campervan, and a sailing yacht, all for less money than the average American mortgage. This is the foundation of The Trifecta. Even if we spent $100,000 on each portion, we'd be coming out ahead, and the idea is to split it all so effectively we are both able to make this a reality for less than half of the cost of a traditional mortgage. This produces seemingly endless possibilities for us and truly embodies the ideal of having more with less. Altogether, we'd gain the whole world for less than the cost of a single unnecessarily sized home. While it'll take time for this dream to manifest into reality, it's only possible because we elected to have more with less, beginning with our Yachtmaster certifications.

At this point, you've seen two different ways to reclaim your life and gain free time for things that are meaningful to you. Having more with less boils down to having the time to work towards your personal potential and becoming the best you can be since you have less of the things that are keeping you from doing so. Ultimately, this involves knowing your purpose, or at least having an idea about what it is. Knowing your purpose then allows you to begin working on personal projects, or passion projects. Personal projects can be thought of as things you would do just for the sake of doing them, meaning it's not about the project's outcome but about the joy you get out of the process and the reasons you have for doing whatever it is in the first place. They don't have to involve money, but it's incredible when you can combine a personal project with increased wealth.

LISTEN TO YOUR INNER CHILD

I've been talking a lot about personal potential and purpose, and I recognize that many people don't know what their purpose is, so allow me to assist. To begin, recognize that the best way to be successful is to build a life (and personal projects) on top of a foundation that is rooted in your purpose. Understanding your purpose involves a certain amount of self-awareness. The best way I know of leading you to your own purpose is by reminding you of your initial life intentions—the thing (or things) you aspired to be throughout your life before the world got hold of you. Whether you know it or not, the inner child within you is still crying out for you to flex your muscles of meaning. Take a few minutes to think about all the roles you've aspired to be over the course of your life. Most importantly, remember what you wanted to be when you were a child.

As you likely know by now, you probably didn't really want to be whatever it was you aspired to be when you were a child; although interestingly, one in seven adults manage to achieve the job they dreamed about when they were children, according to nspcc.org.

Whether you became what you thought you wanted to be or not, what's important is the meaning behind why you chose what you chose. There is an underlying theme beneath every role a child chooses. The role of choice is innately linked to a person's purpose—whatever type of work they will forever find most meaningful and fulfilling. This is how people find things they don't consider work but are still hard work. This is because they do the work for the sake of doing it. It's meaningful to them, so they enjoy it and they get into a state of flow when they are engaged in it. Thus, understanding the meaning behind the role(s) you've sought is the key to unlocking your purpose. For example, a child who aspires to be a doctor will forever find fulfillment in healing and removing suffering from others, a child who aspires to be a teacher will forever find fulfillment in helping others achieve their goals, a child who aspires to be an astronaut will forever find fulfillment in trailblazing new paths for humanity. There is magic in the meaning. Identifying the underlying why in a child's initial job aspiration should be thought of as the foundation for their life's work. Most of the time, it should not be taken literally, but figuratively. In this way, you can retroactively identify your why—the things that will bring you the most fulfillment and enable you to live a life that is extremely meaningful to you. The more meaning you associate with something, the higher quality your work will be in that arena.

To take it a step further, I'll provide you with my analysis of the roles I've personally aspired to, what I take them to mean now, and the personal projects that have evolved from these understandings. Note that these personal projects have all become possible for me since I've traded work projects for personal projects, although I'm not saying you can't have a job and personal projects simultaneously.

Throughout my life, there have been three major roles that I've aspired to. When I was a child, I wanted to be an anthropologist. I found it fascinating that we could learn from our past (where we came from) and understand how we got here by finding and analyzing ancient artifacts. Today, I can tell you that I don't want to spend my time on my hands and knees digging around ancient burial sites, but I'm still motivated to learn and share knowledge about human history because it enables us to experience daily gratitude, and I know that's one of the keys to happiness. I hope my passion for this subject has become evident to you throughout this book, which is a major personal project for me.

The second role I aspired to was a doctor. This was a short period of about two years, but the aspiration was strong, so I must acknowledge it. As someone who didn't especially enjoy school, there was just no way I could've endured another 14 years of it to become a doctor. Thank goodness I didn't. Today I realize that I don't want to be a doctor, but I find great meaning in serving others and helping people eliminate their pain and suffering through self-enrichment, self-awareness, and reclaiming their lives. This purpose is manifested in this book, as well as my two solutions to attaining financial freedom contained in this book.

The third role I aspired to (that I did achieve on paper) was an engineer. I spent most of my teenage years and young adult life thinking that I wanted to be an engineer, but after having the option to practice engineering professionally, I can tell you that I would never want to be locked in an office like that performing calculations and design services all day long. In hindsight, I was attracted to the idea of being able to create a better tomorrow. After much thought, I found that this was closely related to my archeological aspiration, although instead of being completely fascinated by the past, this time it was the future. From this realization came my understanding of my obsession with the concept of human evolution and my determination and motivation to impact it positively. This brought me to the premise that widespread financial freedom is the next step in human evolution, which is why I've worked so hard to create two solutions to help us get there. You see, none of this would've been possible without recognizing these things ultra-meaningful. It wasn't a motivational struggle to produce these solutions, although it did require years of hard work and sacrifice to bring them to fruition. If I had not intentionally linked my personal projects to my understanding of my purpose, these projects would likely still be just a couple of good ideas. So, I implore you:

- identify the type of work you find most meaningful (your why);
- tie it to a personal project;
- and begin it—there you will find your success.

I assure you that the world needs your personal project(s), and you just can't comprehend what they might turn into until you get going. Another great way to identify your purpose is by asking yourself two questions:

1. What would you do if you knew you couldn't fail?
2. What would you do with your life if money weren't an issue?

HAVING MORE WITH LESS = MENTAL HEALTH

At this point in my life, I have both more and less than I have ever dreamed of. I have more passion, more fulfillment, more meaningful work, more family time, more me time and more clarity than I imagined I could have, while having fewer material possessions than most people would aspire to have in our highly consumerist culture. I also have less stress, fewer worries and pointless obligations (meetings), fewer excuses, and less negativity than I thought was possible. I'll admit that having more with less is quite a counterintuitive concept, but it sure pays to master it. As odd as it sounds, it's almost like my intuition knew my true potential and freedom were waiting for me to get rid of all my stuff and begin to live with less. It was obvious how my inner space and my mind began to declutter as I eliminated my possessions one by one. Perhaps the biggest thing I gained from elimination was the time and opportunity to invest in myself and really get to discover who I am. It took time to realize what I'm here for, where I come from, what makes me unique, what makes me feel alive, and what ways I've been given to provide value to others. That's a huge part of making the change to having more with less. Within a year of living with less, my worries almost completely disappeared. I felt liberated and free, almost like an entirely different person who, for the first time, was able to breathe deeply, stand up straight, and think clearly. What do I even have to worry about anymore? How to get from Australia to Europe quickly? How to build a digital empire? How to make the largest possible positive impact? How to live my version of the American Dream? How to be the best friend and family member I can be? These are some of my new concerns.

Likewise, people that are tiny-home living enjoy a more relaxed, simpler, and slower pace of life than their traditional home living counterparts. It's simple, they have less, so they have less to worry about. This ultimately equates to more peace, less stress, and a higher quality of life. There's less worrying about how they're going to find the time to clean the whole house or how they're going to afford the electric bill this month. They don't have to set time aside to sort through holiday decorations and then distribute them across 2600 square feet multiple times per year. Tiny homes are also generally more integrated with the outdoors. This enables tiny home residents to live more in line with our hunter-gatherer ancestors. You learned in Chapter 6 that our hunter-gatherer ancestors led fairly fulfilled lives, and I believe that any way we can build on their success is a positive thing.

Another surprising benefit of tiny-home living is better quality sleep. Since tiny home bedrooms are typically just a bed, they're more likely to be absent of stimulating things such as TVs, cell phone charging stations, and even light in some cases. Lastly, a tiny home necessitates that couples and families spend more time together. This builds relationships and is a blessing, but it can also be a challenge. Avoiding interpersonal problems isn't as easy in small spaces, but tackling problems head-on may be best in the long run. Accordingly, one of the most promising reported outcomes of tiny-home living is improved communication, which helps build stronger relationships. These are all great benefits of having more with less.

FAMILY LIVING IN TINY HOMES

A common question about tiny living is the question of how it works for a family with children. I am not a parent yet myself, so I can't provide firsthand experience of being in the situation, but the short answer is that with proper design and planning, tiny-home living can be a recipe for a superb childhood and a happy family. As discussed in Chapter 3, having a large family home with a separate room per child often means both parents must have full-time jobs to pay for the space. Consequently, the children spend their days being cared for by others. Comparatively, families that live in tiny homes are often debt-free with drastically lower overheads than their traditional living counterparts. This enables the parents to work fewer hours and spend much more time with their children. Naturally, the elimination of space produces greater financial resources that can be channeled into more meaningful areas such as family trips and discovering passions associated with hobbies, sports, and other extracurricular activities. In this way, personal projects can begin at a much younger age for children, and they'll benefit from having their parents guide and assist them along the way.

Proper design and future planning are the two keys to having a tiny home meet the demands of family life. In most cases, the basic needs of children are automatically satisfied by the common spaces of a tiny home such as the kitchen, bathroom, and living room area. The difficulty generally lies in finding a place for children to have their own privacy and their own space to sleep. Fortunately, when they're young, children are generally small, so you can get quite creative when designing spaces for them within tiny homes. There is a great sense of comfort that comes from small spaces, and kids love having their own little nooks to call their own, regardless of how it compares in size to a traditional bedroom. On the other hand, with space at such a premium, sometimes it's not always possible to create separate spaces for adults and children within the four walls of a tiny home. Sometimes this means kids' sleeping spaces are in communal areas that transform into bedrooms at night. Even in this case, it's possible to design some form of separation into the home such as hanging curtains or pop-up dividers.

Regardless of the sleeping situation, just like adults that subscribe to tiny living, children who grow up in tiny homes tend to spend more time outdoors. This can have amazing benefits on a child's development in both the short term and the long term. Accordingly, a recent study of more than 900,000 people performed by researchers at the Aarhus University in Denmark discovered that kids who spend more time outside playing during their childhood are less likely to develop psychiatric disorders as adults. This is surely a huge benefit associated with children living tiny.

Obviously, children's needs change as they grow older. This is where the second key to family tiny living comes into play—future planning. If you're going to successfully live in a tiny home as a family, you must understand that the same solution that works when the child or children are young will not be the same solution that works when they get to a certain age. In other words, your tiny home setup when you have young kids will not be your "forever solution." Whatever solution you come up with will inevitably be based on individual preferences and family dynamics, but I want to share a few clever ways that I've seen families navigate life as their children grow. When the home has a permanent location, there are many more options available. In this scenario, it's possible to create a separate structure for your children's bedroom(s). This way, the children can still utilize all the basic amenities of the main house, but they gain their own space and privacy, which is especially important as children age. Oftentimes the separate structure is just a simple space with a bedroom and its own bathroom. This allows a family to build or add on based on demand rather than purchasing a four- or five-bedroom home without the immediate need for the space.

Another amazing way to meet a child's needs as they grow is by adding an additional tiny home to the lot. This can work if you have your own land or if you live the mobile life, but it's surely easier if you have a permanent residence. If you build or buy an additional tiny home for your child to live in, they gain their own space right next to you, and you're gifting them a permanent residence, which virtually removes their cost of living from their adult life (if they'd like). If they elect to go to college or live elsewhere, you can then rent the additional tiny home to create a source of passive-income, and you still retain the possibility of gifting the home to your child in the future. Only do this if you want to win the Parent of the Decade Award.

FLIPPING THE SCRIPT

Since I've been traveling full-time, it's been no surprise that I've gotten to interact with many retired folks. As you can imagine, retired people make up many of the people out traveling the open road, and I thoroughly enjoy gaining their wisdom and life insights. After many conversations, I'm confident that many of them understand the concept of having more with less. After all, they're mostly in Q4 of their respective Clock of Life, and they have strong opinions about how someone can live a life they will look back on fondly. I've been able to use these people as a sounding board to verify that I'm on the right path, or at least living a life that I'll be able to look back on without regrets. These are the people I get to ask the tough questions to, and I look at these conversations as opportunities to talk to them about my life and my choices. The responses have been unanimous. After sharing my situation and choices, there's no better thing to hear than, "Wow, if only we could have done that in our late twenties."

A large part of my message is flipping the script and not working for 40 years just to start enjoying life fully in Q4 and letting people know that there are other life possibilities. You can create income in a way that doesn't require your constant attention, you can live however you want to, and you can have as much or as little as you want. All these choices directly influence your ability to look back on your life and tell yourself that you left nothing on the table, you did everything you wanted to do, you saw everything you wanted to see, and you gave your short time on earth your best shot.

Now that we've discussed many of the benefits of having more with less and tiny-home living, we must take a critical look at some of the issues that are preventing millions of people from being able to claim their version of the American Dream within the Tiny Home Movement. In the following chapter, I'll explain two roadblocks in depth and provide a solution that will enable many people to reclaim their lives and begin living a life more consistent with our Founding Fathers' intent.

CHAPTER 11

It's Time for Change

YOU'LL BE OLD AND YOU NEVER LIVED,
AND YOU KIND OF FEEL SILLY TO LIE
DOWN AND DIE AND TO NEVER HAVE LIVED,
TO HAVE BEEN A JOB CHASER AND NEVER
HAVE LIVED.

Gertrude Stein

As I've briefly touched on in past chapters, my professional experience immediately following college consisted of four years of project management in engineering and commercial construction at the national level. This is where I met the other half of The Trifecta originally, and where we quickly became best friends. Between the two of us, we had projects across the country from New York City to Portland. For our respective projects, we were each solely responsible for managing every aspect of a building's construction from concept to completion. This means we handled communications and permitting with the cities, the entirety of the design process (civil, architectural, structural, etc.), and the hiring and firing of contractors while managing the ongoing construction process, the project's finances/budget, and the building's turnover to our clients upon completion. We were a one-stop-shop for design, permitting, and construction services. Both of us wore many hats and gained extremely valuable experience. Between the two of us, our projects in 2018 totaled more than $25 million dollars. These were not small operations, so I'm sure you are beginning to understand how I became burnt out. As we were sitting on a stunning beach on the coast of Spain and beginning to work on our dream known as The Trifecta, we had a shocking realization. A realization that I believe will translate into financial freedom for many people across America.

Almost 6 million people are following the top 38 tiny-home-related Instagram accounts alone. Do you know how many households are tiny-home living in the U.S.? Just 10,000. This equates to just 0.17% based on Instagram interest alone. So, how can there be so many people be interested but so few people living the dream? We found two equally important roadblocks when we first began our own tiny home research for The Trifecta. The first is the fact that the process to go tiny is difficult, confusing, and complex. Between coordinating a land purchase, navigating city zoning requirements and restrictions, building-code requirements, and the utility work to mesh it all together, a person is in for quite a headache. We have the professional background, degrees, and experience that is well suited for this type of endeavor and even we found it frustrating, at first. Navigating all the components initially proved difficult, and our experience helped us realize that the process will be different for every single county and city across the U.S. Thankfully for us, we have tons of experience understanding local codes and restrictions, and communicating with city officials to find amicable solutions for both parties. Unfortunately, this doesn't solve the second major roadblock—most cities and counties don't allow tiny homes, due to the structure's impermanence and the official minimum square footage requirement. This is one of the most ridiculous and life-limiting rules that exists in modern society, and it's something that we intend to help change.

THE STRUGGLES OF GOING TINY

Let's dive further into roadblock number one, the general difficulty standing in the way of millions of people trying to go tiny and effectively change their lives. Remember, these are people who want to eliminate the need to work unfulfilling jobs, people who want to simplify their lives by having more with less, and people who want to spend more time doing what they love instead of sacrificing their time for their space. Note that tiny homes are glorified luxurious RVs, and most are built on top of flatbed trailers that make them completely mobile, just like a travel trailer. The first component people generally try to figure out is whether they want to be fully mobile (constantly on the move) or on a plot of land where they can "permanently" place their home. This is a lifestyle decision and varies widely from person to person and family to family. For the people wanting to retain mobility, a vehicle capable of towing their tiny home when they want to move to the next spot is also needed. These people generally don't have to worry about city and county restrictions, since they are not in a place for long enough to require registration. On the other hand, the people wanting to establish a permanent home base don't need a vehicle, since they don't plan to move their home after it is initially placed. In this case, the entire can of worms opens in terms of possible city restrictions. These people generally try to figure out where they want to put their tiny home and whether it will be formally allowed there. Many quickly give up when they get into the building and zoning codes or try talking with a city official. They don't know what they're looking for, and they don't know how to present their case, so they get frustrated and go back to dreaming about tiny living on Instagram. Sound familiar?

The second piece of the first roadblock that people tend to struggle with is the utility portion. This is much easier to figure out for the people that want to move regularly, since tiny homes function like a typical RV. In most cases, the places people park temporarily are already setup for RVs, meaning they have a temporary sewer connection, a 240-

volt electrical connection, and water service. These services are more difficult to figure out when wanting to establish a permanent home base since these people need to figure out how to get all these utility services wherever they want to park their home permanently. For these people, questions quickly arise about how to get sewage service, water service, electricity, and internet. Fortunately, in both cases (nomadic vs. static) there are multiple ways to eliminate the need for these services in the traditional sense. For example, instead of having to go through the city and the local electrical provider for a hard-wired connection, a tiny-home owner can elect to have a solar system. Instead of having to engage the city to hookup the tiny home to the city's sewer system, a tiny-home owner can select a combination of composting and a gray-water rock filtration system, and instead of having to contact the city and the local water service provider, a tiny-home owner can elect to have a fresh-water tank that collects rain water and/or gets filled by a water provider every few months.

These abilities create the question of whether someone needs to contact the city for approval in the first place. My professional recommendation is to get written approval before placing your tiny home permanently, but I will tell you that many people elect to go off-grid. They can get away with this, since they don't really need anything from the city. Of course, this is exactly what cities are afraid of. In these cases, cities are missing out on valuable tax dollars they need to function and provide the services that their community needs. Historically, cities haven't allowed impermanent homes or homes under a certain square footage because they didn't want to attract trailer parks. Because of this, the rules, codes, and regulations are still setup to eliminate the possibility of tiny homes, which as you know, would be an amazing thing for so many people. Since it's not allowed, people are often forced to go around the rules completely, which effectively hurts the city by missing out on tax dollars. Government was created to protect and serve the people, a promise not currently being upheld.

The people want tiny homes! The people want financial freedom! We need cities to step up and create new legislation and change zoning codes to allow for tiny homes, while taxing them appropriately to allow for a mutually beneficial relationship between tiny-home owner and local governments. This starts with city and state officials realizing the potential of tiny-home living, and this needs to happen at the local level, not just the national and state levels.

Positively, this is starting to happen! Most notably, the state of California recently passed a new series of state bills regarding ADU's (accessory dwelling units) and moveable tiny homes. According to the California Department of Housing and Community Development, these 2020 ADU rule changes are statewide in California and all local jurisdictions (cities, counties, etc.) began complying with these new laws January 1, 2020. If a city doesn't create a new Accessory Dwelling Unit Ordinance, state law applies. If a city creates their own ADU Ordinance, it must comply with these new rules. Because of these new state bills, on December 19, 2019, Los Angeles was the first major U.S. city to define and legalize movable tiny homes! This was a huge day for the tiny-home movement, and it has helped establish critical momentum needed in other parts of the country.

BYE-BYE BARRIERS: A FREE TOOL FOR MAKING YOUR TINY-HOME LIVING DREAM COME TRUE

LA's ADU rule was the beginning of the second roadblock's downfall. But what about the first roadblock? How can people overcome the complexity of the process and navigate the three components (land, tiny home, utilities/sitework) necessary to make the change? I'd like to introduce you to version two of The Trifecta—Trifecta Tiny Homes. Trifecta Tiny Homes is a free service that anyone can use to go tiny. When we were initially frustrated while looking to get our original Trifecta started, we asked ourselves, why isn't there an integrated solution that takes care of the entire process from concept to completion? We applied our design and construction expertise to a smaller package and Trifecta Tiny Homes was born out of our own pain as a solution to yours.

Going tiny doesn't have to be complicated, it should be simple. We believe everyone should have the ability to live in a tiny home when they realize that it enables them to have time, money, and liberty simultaneously. We are here to make that a reality and do it in a free and enjoyable way. We leverage our in-house team, our national land partners, and our professional tiny-home builder partners to create a seamless process designed to get you from traditional to tiny as efficiently as possible. Did I mention it's free?

Does this sound like a personal project to you? That's because it is! And getting to work on something that truly matters with my best friend has been a dream come true for both of us. Version two of The Trifecta (Trifecta Tiny Homes) consists of three key components: your perfect property, your dream tiny home, and the utilities design and site work necessary to make it all a reality. Here's how it works:

1. Let us know your dream location, budget, desired number of bedrooms, dream land size, and contact info by submitting the simple form on our website (**www.trifectatinyhomes.com**).
2. Next, you'll receive your Dream Tiny Home Selection Package from us via email within 23 hours. Yes, 23. This package will include tiny home options within your designated budget range and a land questionnaire that gives us the information we need to go to work on the land component. If you can't find a home you like within our current offering, don't worry; together we'll widen the search and find one you love.
3. Once you send us your Land Questionnaire and tiny-home choice from the Selection Package, we'll send you some land options that meet your criteria, budget, and desired location.
4. As soon as we have the land selection and tiny-home selection finalized, together we'll go to work on the utilities and sitework

portion to make sure you get the most efficient design for your dollar and lifestyle preferences.

5. At this point the budget will be finalized, and you'll be able to execute contracts for your land, your new tiny home, and the sitework and utilities necessary to put it all together. We will continue to stand-by until the process is completed, and you are happily moved into your new home with your new set of tiny keys.

If you already have some land or want to live the mobile life, we'll bypass the land portion and go straight into identifying your dream tiny home within your designated budget before we get into the utilities and sitework portion, if necessary. We can't wait to hear from you, and we are so excited about all the wonderful life changing stories and personal projects we are going to help create.

Overall, the second roadblock to tiny living is still at large in America. Most states and cities across the country still have outdated rules regarding impermanent structures and minimum square footage requirements, so I want to provide you with some tools and methods to combat this legally. The more people who are properly informed and can speak to this issue knowledgably, the faster we are going to experience the changes we need to create lasting freedom for many.

The first thing you need to know is there are two types of tiny homes: a tiny home on wheels, legally considered a recreational vehicle (RV), and a tiny home on a foundation, legally considered to be an accessory dwelling unit, or ADU. If you're building a tiny home on wheels, you'll need to register it as an RV with your state. The professional builders take care of this if you go that route, but in most states, a self-built RV will need to be inspected before it gets a license plate.

Building an accessory dwelling unit, however, is more complicated and typically involves permitting a formal design with the local building department. It's also important to learn the difference between building codes and zoning codes. Building codes dictate how a building must be built, while zoning codes dictate where you can build what. You can always apply for a variance to build something outside the established codes. It's best to start the process by calling and speaking to an official at the local planning and zoning department and asking them if they have any of the following:

- Minimum square-footage requirements for new residential construction
- Rules and regulations regarding impermanent structures
- Established zoning requirements for tiny homes

Applying for a variance is the best route to take if you are seeking written approval to establish a permanent tiny-home residence and you find that tiny homes are not allowed due to impermanence or minimum square-footage requirements. The more people applying to local planning and zoning departments for variances associated with tiny homes, the sooner they are going to wake up to the needs of the people.

Another tool we've created to help people go tiny is a comprehensive aid for navigating the utility portion of The Trifecta. It is designed to walk you through the process of deciding how to meet your utility needs and includes the major choices involved for each type of utility service along the way. It also includes average prices associated with each alternative so you can get a full understanding of your options. Additionally, each of the three major utility components (water, power, sewer) comes with a "Trifecta Recommendation," which is what we've found to be the best way to satisfy these needs from a budgetary perspective, a city approval perspective, and a speed of installation perspective. We've done our best to make it as thorough as possible, but it is not entirely all-inclusive. We've seen many creative ways to satisfy utility needs as we've continued to learn more about the tiny-home movement and all the innovative people within it. You can find our utility tool at **www.trifectatinyhomes.com/utility-aid**.

To summarize, the change needed is twofold:

1. Convert all the buzz, interest, and desire surrounding the tiny-home movement into action and change through our Trifecta Tiny Homes Service.
2. Change legislation at the local and state levels so that the original intent of the American Dream can be acquired for those that seek it.

The truth is that the American Dream is more alive today than it has been for decades. But for it to be realized for many, we need government to step up and produce some necessary changes in legislation regarding tiny-home zoning and placement.

The Upshot

THE PERSON WHO SAYS IT CANNOT BE
DONE SHOULD NOT INTERRUPT THE
PERSON DOING IT.

Chinese Proverb

I like to think that our Founding Fathers are smiling down upon us. If we could hear their words, I think they would begin by rejoicing at how far we've come and express sheer amazement at our modern capabilities. They'd high five each other at how prosperous our great nation is, and they'd speak of how lucky we are to have the opportunity to create better, fuller, and richer lives and truly live consistently with their intentions. They'd be in awe of our new individual and collective power, and they'd be ecstatic that we have multiple ways to reach our potential. I think we'd also hear a cautionary tale about how we must continue to shift our focus from our current definition of the Pursuit of Happiness (materiality and unnecessarily large homes) to their definition of the Pursuit of Meaning (what really matters in life). In the end, I think they'd offer encouragement about how we are perfectly positioned to bring about the society they designed and founded more than two centuries ago—a society where people can attain the American Dream.

To honor the Founders' intentions, we must begin with financial freedom at the individual level. When you have your basic human needs met, you're free to follow your own intuition, free to use your unique gifts, and free to serve your purpose. Our Founding Fathers dreamed of a world where people would have the liberty to serve whatever purpose they desire. I'm here to tell you that we've made it; you have the liberty to choose to serve your own purpose or sacrifice your life for someone else's. Whatever you do, don't make your sole purpose paying for your space. It doesn't matter who you are, what you've done, or where you're from: you're meant for more than that.

I challenge you to find something that makes your heart sing and put it at the core of your life. Find something you want to do just for the joy of doing it and begin doing it regularly. Take time to recognize the modern comforts and enjoy your kingdom. Remember that you were created to rule your kingdom, so don't let it rule you. Financial struggles are stressful, but at the end of the day, they're only numbers. Master your mind, and numbers can't hurt you.

Understand the real consequences of accepting debt before you sign up and it's too late. Understand what you or a loved one is committing to with a student loan or mortgage. These are life-limiting decisions that should not be taken lightly. They have 20- or 30-year negative consequences and that is a substantial amount of our lives. You now know that I know the pain associated with mortgage debt, student loan debt, and sacrificing my life for causes that were not of utmost importance to me. Let my story be a lesson to you. Understand that you can still identify what type of work is most meaningful to you and begin it, regardless of where you are on your Clock of Life. Let your inner child speak and slow down enough to listen intently; there you will find your purpose.

When faced with a decision about making a life change, visit the Clock of Life. It will allow you to see your future self and better understand which direction will bring you the most fulfillment as you live your life and look back on your choices. Vow to live a life you're proud of; one that you can look back on without regrets. Vow to give this life your best shot and realize that you're only here for an evolutionary moment. Understand that you won't remember all the times you worked late in the office, all the meetings you attended, or all the tasks you completed to earn the salary checks that were deposited into your bank account over the years.

Realize what you're working towards and understand your life numbers so you can evaluate if the time sacrifices are worthwhile. I want you to know your life numbers like the back of your hand. If you know you're working towards retirement at 65 and understand the sacrifices that come with that choice, then great. At least then you know what you want so that when you meet your goal, you'll be less likely to have regrets: you'll have done exactly what you set out to do. Above all, realize that there is so much more to life than work. Don't be one of the fools who wakes up in old age full of regret because you spent your entire life chasing society's version of success—serving your ego and your bank account. Elect to work on things that will last forever, things that will forever belong to your soul. Create your own version of success and design a life you are excited to call your own. YOU are solely responsible for your own happiness, your version of success, and your version of the American Dream. Start acting like it. Don't settle for less; create more.

Throughout this book I've proven to you both qualitatively and quantitatively that financial freedom is within your grasp. Indeed, financial freedom is now a personal choice. The more people that choose financial freedom, the more people there will be to pave the way for innovative paths forward. You can choose to digitally revolt and change your financial situation by creating passive income. You can choose to ditch tradition and claim liberty for yourself, regardless of your age. You can even redesign your life to have more with less. Instead of merely telling you about these new ways to gain liberty and financial freedom, I've provided you with two solutions to help you get there (Three Sevens and Trifecta Tiny Homes). Whether you decide to utilize them or not is up to you. Only you know what you are passionate about and only you can identify your passions if you don't already know what they are.

Like any good teacher, my door is always open, and I hope that you decide to come knocking. But please, don't put your faith in me; put your faith in yourself. Not only that, invest in yourself so you can become who you know you can be. Give yourself permission to live a big life. Step into who you are meant to be. Stop playing small. You're meant for greater things. To level your life up, you must level yourself up first.

I'm not assigning you any projects; you must assign yourself personal projects. I am beyond grateful to both know what I'm passionate about and to get to work on my passions daily. I didn't just stumble upon them; I intentionally searched for them and identified the things that pulled at my heart's strings to understand what I must do. In a journal entry in late 2018 as I eliminated my apartment and possessions, I realized that the most meaningful form of work in my eyes involves providing amazing value to people without the need to demand money in return. More specifically, to me, the most meaningful work involves acts of kindness that provide value to people that they cannot return materially.

In the journal entry, I wrote about how I must become self-aware of the problems I'd want to solve in the world, and to become receptive of three potential nonprofit ideas. Additionally, I made a five-year goal to either found or join a nonprofit and hold a leadership role with great meaning and impact. This was all before I began my quest for self-enrichment and started traveling full-time. Indeed, I have one more personal project to share with you. It's so near and dear to me, I must confess that I cried my eyes out when I decided to do it while lying in my hammock in the mountains of South Dakota (solitude breeds innovation) almost nine months after writing in my journal about the type of work I find most meaningful.

I decided to create a nonprofit called Ego2Being. Ego2Being supports the terminally ill as they reach their personal potential. The moment a person learns they have a terminal illness, a profound shift takes place inside them. Immediately, that person becomes aware of what really matters—what is most meaningful. Things that seemed of utmost importance yesterday, suddenly become meaningless, while previous regrets begin to resurface. What about the gift that person had for the violin? What became of the passion they once felt to save our environment? Why do these unlived lives return now with such power? Confronted with extinction, all previous assumptions are called into question. What does life mean? Have we lived it right? Are there important acts we've left undone? Words left unspoken? Is it too late? In that instant we learn we will soon die, the seat of our consciousness shifts. It moves from the Ego, to the Being. The world is entirely new, viewed from the Being. At once we see what's important.

Our goal at Ego2Being is to help the mother of two create the charity she's always envisioned, to support the engineer as he writes his novel, and to support the Iraq vet as he gets the education he's always desired. In other words, we support the terminally ill as they realize their purpose and assist them in a personal project before it's too late. The objective of the organization is threefold:

1. Support the terminally ill through a personal project as they reach their potential.
2. Research the possibility of someone extending their lifespan (beyond the medical prognosis) by realizing their purpose and beginning to serve it.
3. Increase collective consciousness by compelling others to work towards their personal potential through stories created from our work.

The stories will be the most obvious examples of people reaching their potential, people wishing they took action sooner, and people who aren't afraid to put it all on the line in the name of limited time. That's the way we all need to think, because we all have limited time and we're all dying—it's just a matter of when.

If you've read this whole book and you somehow still don't believe that financial freedom can change the world, sign-up for our newsletter at **www.ego2being.org** and let me prove to you just how much positive change one person with financial freedom can create. Additionally, 100% of the proceeds from my travel photography sales go to Ego2Being. Please visit **www.austinlaudphoto.com** to view my portfolio.

Wherever you are on your Clock of Life, I wish you well on your quest for self-enrichment, your Digital Revolution, and your pursuit of the American Dream. Please connect with me on **Instagram @ austinlaud**. From there, you can also get to:

- Three Sevens Passive Income Program – **www.777tribe.com**
- Trifecta Tiny Homes – **www.trifectatinyhomes.com**
- Ego2Being – **www.ego2being.org**
- My blog – **www.777tribe.com/blog**
- My photography portfolio – **www.austinlaudphoto.com**

A HYPOTHESIS

Before I leave you, I want to highlight my hypothesis that I've carefully interwoven throughout this book but have not stated explicitly. In Chapter 6, you learned that we still use the scientific method to determine absolute truth. As much of our culture suggests, we must assume a hypothesis could be true until we are without a doubt able to determine it is false. When I pose this hypothesis, pause to recognize the deep space within you that might resonate with it. The fact that I'm able to propose this hypothesis is a testament to just how far we've come as a species. If you've learned nothing else from this book, I hope you've at least acquired some gratitude knowing you are a *Homo sapiens* fortunate enough to be living in the 21st century and beyond. I'm soliciting feedback on this hypothesis in whatever way you feel is appropriate—prove it wrong.

New hypothesis: Heaven is now.

What a time to be alive!

Thanks

Jonah Wolf – Thank you for enriching my life beyond measure. You are the partner that I'd always hoped for, and I'd follow you to the ends of the earth. Your personal potential is unparalleled, and I am beyond excited to see what the rest of life has in store for you and for us. Thank you for joining me on this crazy and rewarding entrepreneurial journey. Here's to doing meaningful work together and having some fun along the way—we're only just getting started.

Dan "Downstairs" Miller – Thank you for being such a supportive and loving friend. You gave me the energy and clarity I needed throughout the entire writing process. I couldn't have produced this book without you. Also, thank you for making me laugh like no other and for continually flying all over the world to meet me just to hang out. I couldn't be more thankful that our paths crossed initially in Dallas.

AJ Laudenslager – Thank you for being my sounding board and my verification that I'm not totally crazy. I'll never forget solidifying many of the ideas contained in this book with you late at night while swinging in those dining chairs on the west side of Gili T in Lombok, Indonesia. You are the best little brother a guy could ask for, and I am so happy to have you as a best friend now that we're adults. Here's to many more years of freedom and fun together.

Alex Laudenslager – Thank you for always providing me with an amazing example to follow. I've always looked up to you and the way that you aim to live your life in a meaningful way. I've been using your pre-game toast of "let's go make some memories" in many situations for years now. Here's to a lifetime of brotherly love and crushing our goals.

Taylor Ray – Thank you for being the most loyal friend a guy could ever ask for. You've been my best friend since third grade, and I can't imagine going through life without you. I thoroughly appreciate all our deep conversations over the years that have helped me solidify what I want out of this life and what value I provide. Your thirst for meaning is contagious, and I've never met anyone with a heart as big as yours.

Coach Jon Loudermilk – Thank you for showering me with so much fatherly love and encouragement when I needed it most. I can't thank you enough for the pure positive energy, love, and enthusiasm that you poured into me over the years. You showed me what it means to be a man of strength, and you truly embody what it means to be a loyal friend, a strong partner, an accountable teammate, and an unconditionally loving father. I've never met someone so powerful yet so humble.

Coach Michael Dodd – Thank you for being my "dad away from home" during my high-school years. You showed me how to be an amazing husband, leader, father, servant, and competitor. I'll always remember our one-on-one time together as life-altering, and I thoroughly appreciate the Godly example that you consistently set for me. You truly impacted my life positively, and I can honestly say I don't know where I'd be today without your influence and direction. You are no doubt one of the most special coaches I've ever had the pleasure of knowing.

Jimmy Span – Thank you for encouraging me as a leader and giving me the opportunity to serve a great purpose at a young age. I've always had so much respect for you as a man and as a leader, and I hope that one day people will look at me the way I've looked at you.

Margie and Karl Schraer – Thank you for supporting me like I was your own. Your home was always such a happy and fun place for me to be. I am so grateful for the food you put in my belly, the wisdom you shared with me, and most of all, the incredible example of a loving marriage that you set for me and your daughters to follow.

Rob Griffin – Thank you for always being there for me in college. I could always count on you for a friendly smile, a pleasant conversation, and assistance with any issue I could come up with. Your easy going and loving demeanor always gave me comfort, and I will always remember how you treated everyone at Hanszen like they were your own.

Coach Chris Thurmond – Thank you for giving me the mentality of "why not me?" You've helped me realize that if other people are doing the things I want to do, there's no reason I can't find a way to do them too.

Jeff Sher – Thank you for pushing me to be the best I could be and test the limits of what I thought was possible. Without you, I wouldn't have got into Rice, and I would be a totally different person than I am today without that experience.

Coach Melvin Crosby – Thank you for teaching me the value of servant leadership. I'll never forget how the guys looked up to you. You taught me that it can be extremely rewarding to serve people knowing they can't repay you in the same way. I still think about your daily acts of kindness through service. In fact, I believe that witnessing them throughout high school has helped me realize the same sort of passion within myself. Thank you so much for putting meaning first.

References

99firms.com. "Affiliate Marketing Statistics to Help You up Your Game in 2020" **https://99firms.com/blog/affiliate-marketing-statistics/#gref.**

Abigail Hess. "This is the age most Americans pay off their student loans" **https://www.cnbc.com/2017/07/03/this-is-the-age-most-americans-pay-off-their-student-loans.html**

Adams, James Truslow. *The Epic of America*

Boston, MA: Little, Brown, and Company, 1931

"Accessory Dwelling Units (ADUs) and Junior Accessory Dwelling Units (JADUs)" **https://www.hcd.ca.gov/policy-research/AccessoryDwellingUnits.shtml**

Becker, Joshua. "21 Surprising Statistics That Reveal How Much Stuff We Actually Own" **https://www.becomingminimalist.com/clutter-stats/**

Carson, Ben. "U.S. Department of Housing and Urban Development" **https://archives.hud.gov/remarks/carson/speeches/2017-06-27.cfm**

Chaturvedi, Aditya. "Do You Know How Many Satellites Are Currently Orbiting around the Earth?"

https://www.geospatialworld.net/blogs/do-you-know-how-many-satellites-earth/

Curtin, Melanie. "94 Percent of Millennials Say This Is Their No. 1 Life Goal (It's Not Career or Love)" **https://www.inc.com/melanie-curtin/94-percent-of-millennials-say-this-is-their-no-1-life-goal-its-not-career-or-love.html**

Fay, Bill. "Key Figures Behind America's Consumer Debt" **https://www.debt.org/faqs/americans-in-debt/**

Ferris, Timothy. *The 4-hour Workweek: Escape 9-5, Live Anywhere, and Join the New Rich* Crown Publishers, 2009

Field, Anne. "Millennials Want Companies Mixing Mission and Money" **https://www.forbes.com/sites/annefield/2017/12/11/millennials-want-companies-mixing-mission-and-money/#5dfa75bf2cf1**

Flood, John C. "History of Plumbing Timeline: The Invention of Indoor Plumbing" **https://www.johncflood.com/blog/general/history-of-plumbing-timeline**

Harari, Yuval N. *Sapiens: A Brief History of Humankind*

First U.S. edition. ed. New York, NY: HarperCollins Publishers, 2015

Kathleen Howley. "U.S. mortgage debt hits a record $15.8 trillion" **https://www.housingwire.com/articles/u-s-mortgage-debt-hits-a-record-15-8-trillion/**

Kristine Engemann, Carsten Bøcker Pedersen, Lars Arge, Constantinos Tsirogiannis, Preben Bo Mortensen, and Jens-Christian Svenning "Residential green space in childhood is associated with lower risk of psychiatric disorders from adolescence into adulthood" **https://www.pnas.org/content/116/11/5188**

LaVoie, Laura. "Tiny Houses on Gizmodo and Top 4 Tiny Living Objections" **https://tinyhousetalk.com/tiny-houses-gizmodo-4-tiny-living-objections/.**

Marshall, Catherine. *A Man Called Peter*

New York, NY: McGraw-Hill, 1951

NitroCollege.com. "Average Student Loan Debt in the U.S. 2019 Statistics" **https://www.nitrocollege.com/research/average-student-loan-debt**

nspcc.org. "Most Popular Childhood Dream Jobs Revealed"

https://www.nspcc.org.uk/what-we-do/news-opinion/uk-dream-jobs-revealed/

Philip Bump. "48 percent of millennials think the American dream is dead. Here's why" **https://www.washingtonpost.com/news/the-fix/wp/2015/12/10/48-percent-of-millennials-think-the-american-dream-is-dead-heres-why/**

Pressfield, Steven. *The War of Art*
Black Irish Entertainment, 2002

Qualman, Darrin. "Home Grown: 67 Years of Us and Canadian House Size Data"
https://www.darrinqualman.com/house-size/

Reed, Eric. "What Is the Average Retirement Savings?"
https://www.thestreet.com/retirement/average-retirement-savings-14881067

Richard G. Klein. *The Human Career: Human Biological and Cultural Origins, Third Edition*
Chicago, IL: University of Chicago Press, 2009

Robert J. Shiller. "The American Dream Is Back"
https://www.nytimes.com/2017/08/04/upshot/the-transformation-of-the-american-dream.html

Selingo, Jeffrey. "Higher Education Is Headed for a Supply and Demand Crisis"
https://www.washingtonpost.com/news/grade-point/wp/2018/01/27/higher-education-is-headed-for-a-supply-and-demand-crisis/

Stanford. "Steve Jobs' 2005 Stanford Commencement Address"

YouTube Video, 15:04. Posted [March 2008]
https://www.youtube.com/watch?v=1i9kcBHX2Nw

Teddy Nykiel. "Current Loan Interest Rates and How They Work" **https://www.nerdwallet.com/blog/loans/student-loans/student-loan-interest-rates/**

"The Underemployment Big Picture"
https://www.payscale.com/data-packages/underemployment

Thomas, Lauren. "Amazon Says This Year's Prime Day Surpassed Black Friday and Cyber Monday Combined"
https://www.cnbc.com/2019/07/17/amazon-announces-prime-day-2019-results.html

Trachta, Ali. "The Most Popular College Majors"
https://www.niche.com/blog/the-most-popular-college-majors/

"What Is Stress?"
https://www.stress.org/daily-life